Fears in Post-Communist Societies

Praise for *Fears in Post-Communist Societies:*

"Based on a wide range of survey data, the contributors to this volume document the human cost of social change in postcommunist societies. The book is a powerful reminder that culture does not exist in a vacuum, that the social order vests itself in the body, and that human emotions mediate the pace and direction of reform. This important cross-cultural study will be particularly useful to students of comparative politics and post-communist culture."

—*Dmitri Shalin, Department of Sociology, University of Nevada at Las Vegas*

"For hundreds of millions of citizens of the former Soviet bloc, the 'transition' of the past decade has been a monumental leap into the unknown—full of hopes, but also dangers. Under those circumstances, the politics and sociology of fear has assumed a special significance. Through extensive survey results and expert analysis, this innovative volume illuminates this portentous post-Communist phenomenon."

—*Nicholas Eberstadt, Wendt Chair in Political Economy, American Enterprise Institute*

"With their groundbreaking study of the fears and concerns of the transitional societies of the former Soviet Union and Eastern Europe, Shlapentokh and Shiraev have performed a seminal service for both the policy and academic communities. Policymakers and NGO officials have been given a guide to the political and social implications of these fears in order to formulate effective policies toward such states. Scholars and students of transitional societies now have a rich source of data to help them understand the politics of change. Shlapentokh and Shiraev have performed a seminal service with their book."

—*Melvin A. Goodman, Professor of International Security, National War College*

Fears in Post-Communist Societies

A Comparative Perspective

Edited by Vladimir Shlapentokh and Eric Shiraev

palgrave

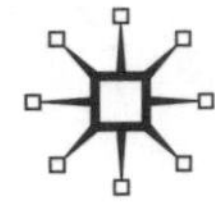

First published 2002 by PALGRAVE™
175 Fifth Avenue, New York, N.Y.10010 and
Houndmills, Basingstoke, Hampshire RG21 6XS.
Companies and representatives throughout the world.

PALGRAVE is the new global publishing imprint of St. Martin's Press LLC Scholarly and Reference Division and Palgrave Publishers Ltd (formerly Macmillan Press Ltd).

ISBN 0–312–29354–2

Library of Congress Cataloging-in-Publication Data
Fears in post communist societies: a comparative perspective / edited by Vladimir Shlapentokh and Eric Shiraev.
p. cm.
Includes bibliographical references and index.
ISBN 0–312–29354–2 (cloth)
1. Social change—Former Soviet republics. 2. Social psychology—Former Soviet Republics. 3. Social change—Europe, Eastern. 4. Social psychology—Europe, Eastern. 5. Post-communism. I. Shlapentokh, Vladimir. II. Shiraev, Eric, 1960-

HN523.F.F4 2002
303.4'0947—dc21

2001048394

A catalogue record for this book is available from the British Library.

Design by Letra Libre, Inc.

First edition: May 2002
10 9 8 7 6 5 4 3 2 1

Printed in the United States of America.

Contents

Preface

This book is addressed to everybody who is interested in European politics, East European studies, and, in particular, post-communist and transitional societies. This volume appeals to political scientists, historians, political psychologists, and sociologists. The book is also contemplated for classroom use as a required reading in comparative politics, international relations, and Russian and Eastern European politics. It can supplement a wide spectrum of university undergraduate and graduate courses.

This book is a result of a 3-year-old cross-national research venture sponsored by the National Council for Eurasian Studies, which has already endorsed the results of the project. The work is based on a series of empirical projects—primarily national pools and smaller surveys—conducted in post-communist European countries in the 1990s and 2000, including Lithuania, Poland, Ukraine, Russia, Belarus, and Czech Republic. The goal of these projects was to investigate and discuss the content of fears, worries, and concerns in post-communist society. In particular, this book discusses various economic fears, fears of catastrophes, worries about internal and foreign enemies, health concerns, and environmental alarms in connection to various aspects of political, social, and economic life in post-communist countries.

This work is based on two types of analysis. The first is an empirical examination of human fears and worries in the designated countries. The methodology of the project is based on multiple-source approaches, including both "snapshots" of opinion polls and longitudinal methods. The researchers were able to consolidate results of public opinion polls with other sources of empirical information, such as small surveys, case studies, and analyses of focus-group discussions. The second type is the exploration of political and social factors that influenced these worries. In this book, the authors gauge sociological traditions that emphasize both rational and irrational elements of the individual's fears.

The book contains a foreword, seven chapters, two essays, an analytical conclusion, and a list of references. Chapter 1 is written by V. Shlapentokh and E. Shiraev and includes a comprehensive description of the nature of human fears, followed by an overview of various societal impacts on fears and worries of the individual in democratic and transitional societies. The chapter also addresses general political, social, and cultural changes during the period of post-communist transition in Europe.

Chapters 2 through 7 are dedicated to six national cases: Russia, Czech Republic, Poland, Ukraine, Belarus, and Lithuania. Chapter 2 is written by a group of leading Russian sociologists and pollsters: Yuri Levada, Vladimir Yadov, Vladimir Shubkin, Grigoriy Kertman, Veronika Ivanova, and Eric Shiraev. Chapter 3 is written by Martina Klicperová-Baker, an expert in political and social transition of contemporary Czech Republic. Chapter 4 is dedicated to analyses of worries in Poland and prepared by Urszula Jakubowska, a senior researcher from the Polish Academy of Sciences. Chapter 5 is written by Vladimir Paniotto, a chief pollster and sociologist from Ukraine, and Eric Shiraev. Chapter 6 is prepared by Larissa Titarenko, a leading sociologist from Belarus. Chapter 7 deals with fears and worries of people in Lithuania and is written by Vladas Gaidys, a sociologist and chief specialist in national public opinion. Chapter 8, written by Samuel Kriger, is dedicated to the study of fears among ex-Soviet immigrants in the United States. The final two commenting essays provide additional comparative information about the dynamics of some people's worries and concerns in two countries: Israel (immigrants from ex-Soviet republics), prepared by V. Aptekman, and the United States, written by David W. Rohde. Chapter 9 is written by Vladimir Shlapentokh and Eric Shiraev as an analytical conclusion to the book.

Please visit the book's website (http://classweb.gmu.edu/eshiraev). There you can find additional tables and charts related to this study. We also provide regular updates of new polls, public opinion studies, and post opinion essays on a great variety of topics related to post-communist countries of the former Soviet bloc.

Sources of Empirical Data

Russia. As part of the original project, two sets of surveys were conducted. Samples for face-to-face interviews were selected from five main regions: Central (Moscow and St. Petersburg), Northern and North-Western, Southern and South-Western, Volga River and the Ural district, and Siberia and Far East districts. In 1996, the sample contained 1,350 persons; in 1999 the national sample was 1,007. Basic surveys were conducted in 1996 and 1999. Additional collected results were based on national surveys conducted by leading polling organizations: VTSIOM and the Public Opinion Foundation.

The Czech Republic. Empirical data presented in this chapter were mostly collected by various polling institutions in the Czech Republic, primarily by the IVVM (Institute for Public Opinion Research)—often coordinated and published under names of M. Rezková, J. Mišovič, V. Jelínek, J.Červenka, further by agencies STEM (Center of Empirical Studies), AISA, GfK, Sofres-Factum and MEDIAN. Where stated, data were borrowed from the reports of CTK (Czech News Agency) or BBC.

Poland. This chapter is based on data obtained from several national surveys conducted by leading Polish public opinion firms, including CBOS. In addition, this chapter uses research data obtained by the author in cooperation with Polish Academy of Sciences and Warsaw School of Advanced Social Psychology.

Ukraine. Between March and May 1998 a study based on the research project "Catastrophic thinking in the modern world" (the "Catastrophes–98" project) was conducted by the Kiev International Institute of Sociology. The data were obtained through face-to-face interviews. The Ukrainian sample included 450 persons and was representative of the adult population (18 and over) of the country. The process of sample selection was multi-staged and based on demographic data published by the State Committee of Statistics. In addition, survey results obtained by various polling organizations were included in the analysis.

Belarus. Several sociological studies and surveys related to the issue of fears, concerns, and worries were used for this case. Most of the data for this chapter were obtained from a series of national surveys conducted by local pollsters or foreign experts (Babosov, 1996; Maysenya, 1996). The first major source is the data from the national survey conducted in Belarus by the International Foundation for Election Systems (IFES) in April-May 1994. Altogether, the sample contained 1,012 adults. For the purpose of this chapter, the results of this survey are compared with the results of the similar IFES Ukrainian national survey conducted in June 1999 (12,000 respondents; see Ferguson, 1999) and surveys conducted in the 1990s by the Center for Political and Social Research, and private firms Novak and NISEPI (Independent Institute for Social, Political, and Economic Research). The second major source of information is the Belarus national survey conducted in May 1999 by the United States Information Agency with a national adult sample of 1,000 people (USIA, 1999; Titarenko, 1999).

Lithuania. The main attitudinal study was based on multistage random sampling, for the designing of which, the 1996 data of Lithuanian Statistical Department were used. To guarantee the proportional representation of population from different regions, the country was divided into five regional strata. The number of respondents in each stratum was proportional to its population size. First stage of sampling included all largest cities (the number of respondents in a stratum is proportional to population size), 11 regions ("rajonas") are selected randomly from the regional stratum (the number of respondents in districts is proportional to the population size). On the second stage, the number of sampling points (100) was distributed among different towns and rural areas. Towns were divided into territorial units. In rural areas districts ("apylinkes") were selected as sampling points randomly. On the third stage, selection of respondents was carried out in towns using the random route procedure.

Russian immigrants. Most data for this chapter have been collected in the research project *Fears in Post Communist Society on the Eve of 2000: Intensity and Impact on Social Life* sponsored by the National Council for Eurasian and East European Research. Altogether, 1,274 immigrants from the New York and Boston areas were interviewed for this chapter between 1996 and 2000.

Vladimir Shlapentokh and Eric Shiraev
Michigan/Virginia/DC, November 2001.

Acknowledgments

No project of this scale could have been realized without the invaluable contributions, backing, and support of scores of individuals and organizations. We are particularly grateful for support from the National Council for Eurasian Studies in Washington, D.C., which made this project possible. A special word of appreciation is due to the administrations, faculty, staff, and students at Michigan State University and George Mason University where we have consistently been provided with an abundance of assistance. We express our gratitude to Charley Greenlief, Vice President of MSU and to Lou Anna Simon, MSU Provost. We also wish to thank the Grant Agency of the Czech Republic for the sponsorship of the projects "Democratic Citizenship" and "Democratic Attitudes in Central and Eastern Europe."

We gratefully acknowledge the helpful advice of Melvin Kohn who provided valuable ideas and gave many critical suggestions at the initial stages of this project. We have benefited from the insightful feedback and advice of colleagues, from the thorough efforts of research assistants, and from the patience and understanding of family members and friends. In particular, we wish to acknowledge Scott Keeter from George Mason University, Richard Sobel from Harvard University, and Vlad Zubok from Temple University. Thank you for encouragement and validation.

We also would like to take this opportunity to acknowledge the tremendous support we received at virtually every stage of this project's development from the editorial team at Palgrave. In particular, we wish to thank David Pervin, Meg Weaver, Ella Pearce, Sonia Wilson, and Matthew Speiser for their support and patience. Finally, we wish to express our mutual feelings of thankfulness to all who contributed to this book.

Chapter 1

Introduction

Vladimir Shlapentokh and Eric Shiraev

Fear cannot be without hope, nor hope without fear.

—*Spinoza (*Ethics, *pt. III, 13)*

On Terminology

This book is an attempt to conduct a comparative analysis of people's fears from a multidisciplinary perspective. Most of fears analyzed in this project were identified through scientific polling. Let us first suggest a few things about terminology used in this volume. Throughout the book, the authors use words such as "fears," "anxiety," "worries," and "concerns." Are they all similar in their meanings? If not, what are the differences? Traditionally in American psychology—and this point of view is generally shared by other international scholars—anxiety refers to a general state of tension and apprehension about the present or future (Barlow, 1999). Fear, on the other hand, is typically associated with an emotional response to a specific object or situation. Anxiety, as compared to fear, is a more free-floating state of emotional response that can or cannot be associated with any specific object. Therefore, in most situations, when an object of worry or concern is identified by a survey respondent, then his or her emotional reaction of tension related to this object and expressed verbally or written down may be called "fear." Moreover, as a matter of convenience, the words "worries" and "concerns" are often used by the authors instead of the word "fears."

On the Psychological Nature of Fears

It is generally accepted that fear is a mental construct that has been shaped during evolution and plays a role of an important signal: If something is feared, the individual should undertake an action to cope with the threat. According to the established psychological "fight-or-flight" model, there are at least two ways of such coping: to fight against the threat or avoid it. If the person is unable to undertake one of these actions, the individual can face numerous unpleasant consequences ranging from chronic stress and frustration to the general state of hopelessness and helplessness. On the societal level, such frustration and hopelessness can influence a wide range of responses, from active political participation to societal alienation and withdrawal.

People's fears can reflect real dangers and real threats. However, fears are also a cognitive construct: They reflect what things and developments people interpret as dangerous and unpleasant. Fear is a result of the mind's work, which is influenced by a variety of social, cultural, ideological, and political factors. What is labeled as dangerous and worrisome in one society may not be a source of fear in others. A ten-percent yearly inflation rate is likely to be viewed a "disaster" by the average American person. For a resident of post-communist Russia or Ukraine, this inflation rate would be seen as very low and as good news about a stabilizing economy.

Working on this project, the authors dealt with human fears that, as it was assumed, were triggered by specific social conditions. The authors were not particularly interested in so-called existential fears, such as the fear of death or the fear of losing a beloved family member: It is very difficult to speculate about the triggers of such fears in a comparative perspective.

A Methodological Concern

Fears also can be different in terms of their intensity and duration. There are constant, persistent, and repetitive fears, which are called chronic. There are acute fears reflecting an extremely tense and apprehensive reaction concerning a specific object or situation: these typically arise under the threat of potentially disastrous events, such as natural cataclysms, terrorism, or mass violence. Mild fears, on the other hand, reflect only some level of apprehensive concern. In a way, all of us have mild concerns about a number of things in our lives. It is very difficult to differentiate different levels of fears in mass surveys. It is hard to ignore a concern that people's reports about their fears may not accurately reflect whether their fears are real or whether they are exaggerated. It is quite possible that people give answers that are considered "politically correct" or acceptable in their country or region. For example, some respondents may say they are "constantly anxious" about what is going on in their home country although they actually experience little anxiety. Pollsters know about the tendency of respondents to exaggerate their concerns about the situation in the whole country—such as crime, environmental problems, corruption—and express less concern about their own city, town, or community. It is also quite possible that during interviews, some respondents were simply cooperating with the pollsters, giving the "expected"—from their point of view—answers.

The authors, believe, however, that the scope and variety of methods used in this project allowed them to make adequate statements about several predominant tendencies and trends in people's worries during more than a ten-year period of post-communist transition.

Fears in the Context of Post-Communist Transition

By the end of the 1980s, millions of people in ex-communist European countries were looking to their future with great optimism and hope. The long-lasting political tyranny of communism, ideological censorship, and oppression seemed to have disappeared for good. Democratic principles of government, market economy, and laws protecting fundamental individual rights were all anticipated to become the guarantors for a worry-free future.

Back in the years immediately following the fall of the Berlin Wall, the topic of this book would not have received much attention from our colleagues in the former Soviet-bloc countries. Although the waters of the societal transition were uncharted, individual fears did not materialize and the euphoric mood of the majority of people, coupled with confidence and great expectations, suppressed individual worries. In many people's minds, the post-communist political and social transition would create only one desirable and seemingly inevitable outcome: societal stability and prosperity for the people.

Since the early 1990s, however, after a few years of reformation, many individuals in these countries began to realize that the existing reality did not match the earlier held expectations. Momentary uncertainties brought back, to some people, nostalgic feelings and serious concerns abut the future. It may be argued that people tend to express anxiety and fear regardless of time, place, or type of society in which they live. In other words, fears are psychological constructs and they are generated continuously despite favorable or unfavorable circumstances in the individual's life. However, in this book, the authors will largely defend the view that people's fears and concerns about the future result primarily from the rational assessment of reality. Particularly, in the examined countries, the post-communist transition process turned out to be extremely difficult and unpredictable. Many people—contrary to their expectations—were not ready for a quick and efficient adjustment to the new social and political conditions in their countries. Individual difficulties and failures to fulfill personal expectations increased their worries and anxiety about the present and the future.

The studied countries shared many common features. Above all, they shared a common legacy of several decades of communist governments. New governments took over the huge public sectors of their national economies, including poorly organized banking, communication, and transportation systems. People of these countries had to deal with outdated or inadequate laws, untested political systems, and the return of the old communist bureaucracy to power. The population of these countries also had to address growing social problems, such as crime and corruption. Ethnic problems became urgent for many post-communist nations. Although unemployment did not constitute a major social problem throughout the 1990s, the population has lost one of the core entitlements of the socialist society, that is, economic security.

Despite these and other similarities, the sampled countries are quite different in terms of their specific economic, social, cultural, and political conditions. Generally, people's fears and concerns do reflect the global developments typical for most post-communist societies under transformation. On the other hand, each country's unique circumstances also affect the way fears are perceived, expressed, and communicated among the population. In other words, people's fears expressed in surveys should be discussed within the context of both "global" and "local" economic, political, and ideological conditions. Can we sort out these general and specific conditions?

Fears in a Comparative Perspective

Throughout this book, the authors attempt to gauge people's fears from a multi-level perspective, assuming that the individual's fears were largely shaped under the influence of several interconnected factors, divided into categories. We should notice that, theoretically, when the researcher attempts to use certain categories for a comparative analysis, the variables within these categories are expected to be homogeneous, there are clear boundaries among the categories, and categories are mutually exclusive. However, this rarely occurs in practice and the distinctions among these levels of comparative analysis are largely conceptual.

At the beginning, the authors looked at the basic socioeconomic conditions in the studied country. On this level, attention was paid to the resources available to the individuals in countries under investigation and to social groups, which had greater access to resources than other groups. Without taking these data into consideration—among them average income, unemployment and poverty rates, and inflation—it is very difficult to gauge many causes of the individual's worries. It is generally expected that the better such conditions are, the fewer worries an individual expresses. Similarly, the individual's fears should increase when socioeconomic conditions become less favorable.

On the next level, the authors paid attention to major social developments and resulting problems in the studied countries. Here attention was paid to factors, such as educational level of various social groups; level of violence and crime in the country; availability and quality of health-care services; the scope of unemployment; the extent of ethnic and religious conflicts in the country; presence of immigrants in the country, and several other factors and conditions.

On the following level, the countries' political landscape was examined. In particular, special areas of attention included: stability or instability of the national government, the extent of public approval of the country's leaders and their opponents; the size and strength of political opposition. It was expected that political instability should enhance people's fears. On the other hand, stability or anticipation of political stability in the country can significantly reduce fears.

Then the authors had to turn to the description of general socio-cultural factors that could have affected people's expressed fears. Attention at this level was paid to the fundamental values and effects of socialization, including religious, moral, and major psychological predispositions in conjunction with particular fears. Special areas of attention include cultural patterns of self-assessment, religious beliefs, historic experience, and general stereotypes related to the government, social institutions, various social groups, and people in general.

Finally, attention was paid to other significant situational factors. On this level, for instance, the researcher determines specific situations and developments that could affect the individual's fears and concerns. For example, some individuals can be predisposed to express worry about almost anything they encounter or are asked about, whereas other people—due to their individual experiences and characteristics—are predisposed to express less worry.

Fears in Sociological Research

Throughout the entire twentieth century, anxiety, along with fear, was a subject of detailed research and serious scrutiny performed by psychologists.

Sociologists, for various reasons, largely neglected fear in their empirical studies. Therefore, the number of sociologists who devoted their empirical studies to the subject of fear, was relatively limited. Pitirim Sorokin's famous book *Man and Society in Calamity* (1968) was mostly theoretical in its approach. Besides this work, there were only a few other publications, which were concerned with the sociology of fear. For example, among the books that stand out there are works of Enrico Quarantelli, Albert Cantrill, and other authors.[1]

Most sociological studies were concerned with post-catastrophic situations and the way societies, organizations, and communities responded to technological or ecological disasters,[2] or how individuals and the public adapt to disasters.[3] The all-encompassing sociological literature on collective behavior and social movements only occasionally investigated the issue of fear. Moreover, fear itself was not generally considered as an individual's emotion, not a social phenomenon. Only in the studies of mob and crowd behavior, fear became the focus of analysis. Furthermore, most studies in this area pertained only to specific extraordinary cases and not to the state of mind of ordinary people in society.[4] Even Barry Glassner's work, *The Culture of Fear* (1999), which was devoted to the fears in America, operated only with casual data and practically ignored survey data. Generally speaking, Samuel Prince's (1920) statement from seven decades ago still holds true today: this topic of fear remains "a virgin field in sociology."

Why Do We Study Fears?

Overall, sociological studies of fears in communist and post-communist societies were relatively scarce. However, several publications on this subject, based on analyses of surveys were released. Many of them dealt with people's perceptions of catastrophic events and calamities as well as economic fears including people's attitudes toward unemployment and poverty.[5] Overall, the repertoire and intensity of people's fears can be used as fine indicators of the political and social stability in society. For this reason, the information about fears can be used to gauge and make assessments about social developments in any country. Both intensity and frequency of reported fears should produce various assumption about the population's feelings and worries about their quality of life.[6] Our knowledge of "transitional" fears is particularly important for a better understanding of the countries in transition.

Notes

1. See Robert Bailey III, *Sociology Faces Pessimism,* The Hague: Martinus Nijhof, 1958; Charles Fritz, "Disaster," in Robert Merton and Robert Nisbet

(eds.), *Social Problems,* New York: Harcourt Brace and World, 1961; Gary Kreps, "Disaster and the Social Order," *Sociological Theory* 3:49–65, 1985; Gary Kreps, "Classical Themes, Structural Sociology, and Disaster Research," in Russell Dynes, Bruna De Marchi, and Carlo Pelanda, *Sociology of disasters: Contribution of Sociology to Disaster Research* (eds.) 357–402, Milan: Franco Angeli, 1987; Samuel Prince, *Catastrophe and Social Change, Based Upon a Sociological Study of the Halifax Disaster,* New York: Columbia University Press, 1920; E. L. Quarantelli, "The Nature and Conditions of Panic," *American Journal of Sociology,* 60:267–75, 1954; E. L. Quarantelli, *Panic Behavior in Fire Situations: Findings and a Model from the English Language Literature,* Newark: Disaster Research Center, University of Delaware, 1981; Marta Wolfenstein, *Disaster: A Psychological Essay,* Glenocoe: Free Press, 1957; Albert H. Cantril, *Hopes and Fears of the American People,* New York: Universe Books, 1971.

2. See Nicholas Demerath and Anthony Wallace, "Human Adaptation to Disaster," *Human Organization,* 16:1–2, 1957; Russell Dynes, "Disaster as a Social Science Field," *National Review of Social Sciences* 13:75–84, 1966; Russell Dynes, *Organized Behavior in Disaster,* Lexington, MA: D.C. Heath: 1970; Russell Dynes, E. L. Quarantelli, and Gary Kreps, *A Perspective on Disaster Planning,* Report series no. 11. Newark: Disaster Research Center, University of Delaware, 1972; Gary Kreps, "The Organization of Disaster Response: Some Fundamental Theoretical Issues," In E. L. Quarantelli (ed.), *Disasters: Theory and Research,* 65–87, London: Sage, 1978; Gary Kreps, "The organization of disaster response: Core concepts and processes," *International Journal of Mass Emergencies and Disasters* 1:439–67, 1983; Irving Janis and Leon Mann, "Emergency Decision Making: A Theoretical Analysis of Responses to Disaster Warnings," *Journal of Human Stress,* 35–48, 1977; Dennis Mileti, Thomas Drabek and J. Eugene Haas, *Human Systems and Extreme Environments,* Boulder: Institute for Behavioral Science, University of Colorado, 1975; Ronald Perry, *Comprehensive Emergency Management: Evacuating Threatened Populations,* Greenwich, CT: JAI Press, 1985; Jerry Rose, *Outbreaks. The Sociology of Collective Behavior,* New York: Free Press: 1982; E. L. Quarantelli, *Disasters: Theory and Research,* London: Sage, 1978; E. L. Quarantelli, *Evacuation Behavior and Problems,* Newark: Disaster Research Center, University of Delaware, 1980; James Wright and Peter Rossi, *Social Science and Natural Hazards,* Cambridge, MA: Abt Books, 1981; A. Mozgovaia, *Sotsialnyie Problemy Ekologii,* vol. 7, Moscow: Institute of Sociology, 1994; Peter E. Hodgkinson and Michael Stewart, *Coping with Catastrophe: a Handbook of Disaster Management,* New York: Routledge, 1991.
3. See Bonnie Green, "Conceptual and Methodological Issues in assessing the psychological impact of disaster," in Barbara Sowder (ed.), *Disasters and Mental Health: Selected Contemporary Perspectives,* Rockville, Md: National Institutes of Health, 1985; J. Eugene Haas and Thomas Drabek, "Community Disaster and System Stress: A Sociological Perspective," in Joseph McGrath

(ed.), *Social and Psychological Factors in Stress,* New York: Holt, Rinehart and Winston, 1970; Thomas Kurian, *The New Book of World Rankings,* New York: Facts on File, 1991; Eli Marks and Charles Fritz, "The NORC Studies in Human Behavior in Disaster," *Journal of Social Issues,* 10:26–41, 1954; Ronald Perry and Michael Lindell, "The Psychological Consequence of Natural Disaster: A Review of Research on American Communities," *Mass Emergencies,* 3:105–15, 1978; E. L. Quarantelli, "What is Disaster? The Need for Clarification in Definition and Conceptualization in Research," In Barbara Sowder (ed.), *Disasters and Mental Health: Selected Contemporary Perspectives,* Rockville, MD: National Institutes of Health, 1985; Daniel Slottje (ed.), *Measuring the Quality of Life Across Countries: a Multidimensional Analysis,* Boulder: Westview Press, 1991; Stuart Walker and Rachel Rosser (eds.), *Quality of Life Assessment: The Key Issues in the 1990s,* Dordrecht: Kluver, 1993; Mike Davis, *Ecology of Fear,* New York: Holt 1998; Rafael López-Pedraza, *Anselm Kiefer: the Psychology of "after the Catastrophe,"* New York: George Braziller, 1996; David R. Marples, *Belarus: From Soviet Rule to Nuclear Catastrophe,* New York: St. Martin's Press, 1996.

4. See Andrew Baum and Yakov Epstein (eds.), *Human Response to Crowding,* Hillsdale: L. Erlbaum, 1978; Erika King, *Crowd Theory as a Psychology of the Leader and the Led,* Lewiston: E. Mellen Press, 1990; J. S. McClelland, *The Crowd and the Mob: From Homer to Canetti,* Boston: Unwin Hyman, 1989; Clark McPhail, *The Myth of the Maddening Crowd,* New York: A. de Gruyter, 1991; E. L. Quarantelli, "The Nature and Conditions of Panic," *American Journal of Sociology,* 60:267–75, 1954; S. Rachman and Jack Maser (eds.), *Panic: Psychological Perspectives,* Hillsdale: Lawrence Erlbaum, 1988; H. Wittchen, "Epidimology of Panic Attacks and Panic Disorders," in I. Hand and H. Wittchen (eds.), *Panic and Phobias,* Berlin: Springer, 1986.
5. Vladimir Shlapentokh, "Fear of the Future in the Modern World: a Russian Case," *International Journal of Comparative Sociology,* 1998, pp. 161–176; Vladimir Shlapentokh, "Catastrophism on the Eve of 2000: Apocalyptic Ideology Between Russia's Past and Future," *Demokratizatsia,* no. 5, winter 1997; Vladimir Shlapentokh, Vladimir Shubkin, and Vladimir Yadov (eds.), *Katastrofichseskoie Soznanie v Sovremennom Mire (The Catastrophic Mind in the Contemporary World),* Moscow: Rossiiskaia Assotsiatsia Nauchnykh Fondov, 1999; Mitev Emil, Veronika Ivanova, and Vladimir Shubkin, "Katastrofícheskoie Soznanie v Bulgarii i Rossis" (The Catastrophic Mind in Russia and Bulgaria), *Sotsiologiuchekie Isseldovania,* no. 10, 1998; Vladimir Shubkin and Veronika Ivanova, "Strakhi v Post Sovietskom Prostrantsve" (Fears in the Post Soviet Space), *Monitoring Obshchetvennogo,* Mnenia, no. 3, 1998; Vladimir Iadov, "Strakhi v Rossii" (Fears in Russia), *Sotsiologicheskii Journal,* No. 3, 1997; Vladimir Shubkin, "Strakh Kak Faktor Sotsialnogo Povedenia," *Sotsiologicheskii Journal,* no. 3, 1997; Vladimir Shubkin, "Ekologicheskia Katastrofa Strashnee Revolutisii" (The Ecological Fears are More Scary than Revolution), *Delovoi Mir,* no. 2, 1997; Vladimir Shubkin, "Struktura Strakhov i Trevog v Sovremnennoi Rossii" (The Structure of Fears and

Anxieties in Contemporary Russia), *Mir Rossii,* no. 2, 1999; Vladas Gaidys, "The Economic Attitudes that Make a Difference," *The Baltic Review (Tallinn),* vol. 13, pp. 45–46, 1997; Vladimir Shubkin, "Attitudes Toward the Economic System in the Baltic States," in *Cultural Encounters in East Central Europe. Report* 98:11, Stockholm, 1998, pp. 61–73; Vladas Gaidys, "Political Activity and Passivity in Lithuania," in *Pilsoniska Apsina. Riga: Filozofijas un Sociologijas Instituts,* 1998, pp. 191–202; Vladas Gaidys, "Political Values: Stability vs. Lability," in A Mitrikas (ed.), *Values in the Time of Changes,* Vilnius: Institute of Philosophy and Sociology, 1999, pp. 74–88; L. Kesselman, and M. Matskevich, "Individual Optimism/Pessimism in the Contemporary Russian Transformation," *Sociology: Theory, Methods, Marketing,* 1998, pp. 1–2, 164–175.

6. It was surprising that, since their emergence in the 1970s, studies on the quality of life, which were oriented to find out what people felt about various elements of their lives, mostly ignored the role of fear and its impact on the quality of life. (See A. Campbell, *The Sense of Well Being in America,* New York: McGraw, 1971; A. Campbell, P. Converse and W. Rogers, *The Quality of American Life: Perceptions, Evaluations, and Satisfactions,* New York: Russell Sage Foundation, 1976; Frank Andrews (ed.) *Research of the Quality of Life,* Ann Arbor: The University of Michigan, 1986, pp. 1–2; E. Allard, *A Frame of Reference for Selecting Social Indicators,* Helsinki: Comentationes Scientarum Socialium, 1972; World Quality of Life Indicators, Santa Barbara: ABC-CLIO, 1989; Robert Lauer, "Social problems and the quality of life," Dubuque: Brown, 1982).

Chapter 2

Russia: Anxiously Surviving

Yuri Levada, Vladimir Shubkin, Grigoriy Kertman, Veronika Ivanova, Vladimir Yadov, and Eric Shiraev

From a historical viewpoint, the period from 1992 to the early 2000s was incredibly short. Yet these years were filled with a remarkable set of dramatic events, and, for this reason, have few parallels in Russian history. These were years of change and turbulence, of people's raised hopes and of growing anxiety about the future. An aftershock that followed the break-up of the Soviet empire was marked by economic collapse and hyperinflation, trailed by the constitutional crisis of 1992–93, the culmination of which was President Yeltsin's use of military force to disband the parliament inherited from the Soviet era. It was a period marked by the left-wing opposition's victories in the legislative elections of 1993 and 1995 and the dramatic electoral campaign of 1996 that kept Yeltsin in the Kremlin office for three-and-a-half years of his second term. (Yeltsin's reign ended with the transfer of power to his handpicked successor, Vladimir Putin). During this period, Russia had fought several undeclared wars, the most devastating of which was the conflict in Chechnya. This war officially began in December 1994 but had actually started months prior and dragged into the new millennium. A devastating financial crisis of 1998 had a profound sobering effect on the remaining few optimists, who believed in a fast, sound, and irreversible economic recovery of the country.

Social transition is never a painless process. During the 1990s, Russia had to be reassembled in every sense: as an economic and military power, a multiethnic state, a legitimate government, and as a democracy. Unfortunately, the problems of dismantling the command economy and stabilizing its new market structure turned out to be daunting. The building of a new civil society was slowed down by privation and lawlessness. Political restructuring did not necessarily lead to democratization. Most importantly, property and power were changing hands in Russia; thus various groups put their own interests above national priorities (Shlapentokh, 1996; Glad and Shiraev, 1999). Also, Russia's old script as an international actor had to be rewritten. This process was long, complicated, and controversial. Russian leaders had a hard time coping with a status as an ex-superpower and never planned to give up their gargantuan goals. After NATO's eastward expansion in the mid-1990s, the wars in Bosnia and Kosovo, and the 1999–2001 military campaign in Chechnya, an old image of a foreign threat was brought back in the area of public debate (Shiraev and Zubok, 2001).

All developments mentioned earlier and many others suggest that the ascendance of Putin to the highest Russian office and his first years in power signified on one hand Russia's strive for change by achieving stability and certainty. On the other hand, such a change was meant to be achieved by the preservation of the status quo.

Popular Disillusionment

The spread of fear and social pessimism in the minds of many people in post-communist Russia was, in many ways, determined by the country's long economic crisis, inflation, social and political instability, widespread corruption, and rampant crime. An optimist could argue that the Russian transformation should have given people a chance to have a voice in political affairs, boost their interest in political life, and stimulate a growing sense of control over the future—a set of developments aimed to reduce people's worries. Gorbachev's policy of liberalization in the mid-1980s seemed to signal the beginning of a true democratization in the country. The level of political participation grew among all social groups, particularly among the Russian urban middle class (Yuriev, 1992).

Nevertheless, initial enthusiasm morphed into political apathy and skepticism. With few exceptions, the level of direct political participation plummeted. For example, fatigue and indifference, according to VTsIOM polls conducted between 1992 and 1995 were reported in 40 to 55 percent of the Russian population (*Moscow News,* 1996, January 19). Popular disillusionment with the course and outcome of the reforms was demonstrated in a number of opinion polls (White et al., 1997; Wyman 1997). As some analysts pointed out, general uncertainty and anxiety about the future were closely associated with people's failure to control the present (Gozman and Etkind 1992). In the mid-1990s, according to surveys, only a small fraction of Russians said that they looked to their future with confidence (Shlapentokh, 1996). A 1995 survey showed that those people who were not satisfied with their lives outnumbered the satisfied by a ratio of eight to one (*Segodnia,* 1995, 2 August). Themes of social disasters and cataclysms were frequently discussed in the media (Shakhnazarov 1996; Grushin 1994). The expression of nostalgic feelings and longings for the past became very common. Opinion polls show that, in the 1990s, people became increasingly nostalgic for pre-Perestroika times, in particular for the Brezhnev era, which they are likely to prefer to what is going on today. When asked to name the years they thought were the hardest in their lives, 65 percent named the period from 1996 to 1999, with 33 percent reporting 1991–1995. The first and second halves of the 1990s were thought to be the best by 7 percent and 8 percent, respectively. These opinions were voiced primarily by younger people, who were small children before the 1990s. A mere 3 percent said life was better under Gorbachev; 48 percent of those surveyed suggested that life was better under Brezhnev, the Soviet leader who died in 1982 (The Public Opinion Report, 1999).

Self-assessments and comparisons made by Russians reveal their pessimism. When respondents were asked to compare themselves to other fellow Russians, 85 percent viewed themselves as belonging to the "lower" part of society. (A January 2000, VTsIOM poll contained the following statement: Consider a ten-point scale, in which "10" represents the best-off, and "1" represents the worst-off. Answer the following questions.) More than 46 percent gave self-evaluations ranging from "1" to "3," suggesting they belonged to the worst-off part of Russian society. At the same time, according to the results of this survey, 75 percent of respondents were convinced that they deserved to belong to the best-off. Only 15 percent expressed an opinion that they should indeed belong to the worst off. It follows that the majority of Russian citizens are firmly convinced that the principle of social justice was alien to their society, because their personal well-being had very little to do with their personal merit.

Moreover, 74 percent of people believed that they were paid less then they deserved (8 percent said they are paid more than they ought to earn). Almost 63 percent of respondents suggested that "hard work is not rewarded in our country," whereas only 16 percent held the opposite, optimistic view (ESP, 1997). From an individual standpoint, if one person believed that he or she "deserved" to be at a higher level of accomplishment, but was not, there must be some forces that prevented this individual from getting what he or she deserved. In Russia, such beliefs were generally based on a popular view that the overall quality of life in society depends on the actions of federal and regional authorities; those who have power are in the position to take major responsibility for the entire country (Levada, 1999; Diligensky, 1997).

In the context of the widespread social pessimism, what kinds of emotions were prevailing in Russians during the transitional years? Some surveys provide information about people's evaluations of their own feelings. (See table 2.1.)

In the period from 1994 to 2000, VTsIOM (Russian Center for Public Opinion Research) measured—both on monthly and yearly bases—various self-assessments of the prevailing mood in Russian residents.

As you can see from table 2.1, the prevailing sense of fear was mentioned—with some consistency—by approximately one out of every ten respondents. There were occasional "hikes" in the expression of fear during especially difficult and tense periods, such as September 1998, the first month following the devastating financial collapse of the Russian markets. Right after this crisis took place, the Public Opinion Foundation (1998) asked people to estimate to what extent the situation influenced their lives. As a result, 50 percent gave the following response: "It has become so bad that we don't know how to live." Another 30 percent answered: "The situation has become much worse, but we are able to bear it." Somewhat optimistic responses were chosen by only 18 percent. For the six-year period, the tense state of their mood was mentioned by four people out of every ten, with only a slight decrease in January 2000, right after Putin was appointed acting president.

In September 1999, Public Opinion Foundation asked a national sample a question: "What concerns you the most?" People were given an opportunity to assess two categories of problems: One was about the country in general and the other was about the individual's personal life. Expressing their opinion about Russia, 46 percent mentioned soaring prices and impoverishment. Crime was suggested in 32 percent of responses. Twenty-four percent said threat of mass unemployment was their prime concern. Issues such as threats of civil war, ethnic conflicts, and threat of famine

Table 2.1 Assessment of Own Mood for the Last Few Days. Mean Scores. Source: VTsIOM, 1994–2000

What point on this scale best describes your current feelings?	*1994–1996**	*1997*	*1998*	*1999*	*Jan. 2000*
[I experience] fear	10	11	12	12	10
[I feel] excellent	3	4	4	3	5
[I feel] normal, calm	36	38	34	36	45
[I feel] tense	41	40	43	41	33

*Mean scores for three years

were each mentioned by 23 percent of survey respondents. Every fifth person suggested "economic crisis" in the country. On the personal level, financial difficulties were mentioned by 58 percent of people. Fear for children (and grandchildren) came in the second place: 39 percent said that this issue concerns them most. Hopelessness and lack of security were named by 29 percent of Russians. About one-quarter of Russians (24 percent) were concerned about their own state of health, as well as the health of their relatives (28 percent).

A survey conducted by the Public Opinion Foundation (1998; Survey Reports Series, June 3, n. 49. p. 22) revealed that a substantial majority of population—71 percent—admitted they were "constantly anxious" about what was happening in Russia at the moment and another 18 percent suggested they were "sometimes anxious." Only 2 percent replied they were not anxious at all.

In 1999 VTsIOM (Levada, 1999b) asked Russians to answer a question: "What feelings have appeared and grown stronger in yourself and among people you deal with over the last few years?" Twenty-nine percent suggested "fear" was getting stronger in other people and 18 percent felt the same about their own fear. "Despair" in others was mentioned by 37 percent, and 26 percent mentioned this feeling in themselves. However, the most common answers were "weariness, indifference." These feelings were recognized as growing by 52 percent of respondents when they referred to other people and by 38 percent referring to themselves. Remarkably, "sense of liberty" and "confidence in tomorrow" were mentioned by a very small proportion of population. For example, only 6 percent expressed an opinion that their confidence in tomorrow grew, and 3 percent said that confidence raised in others. The growing personal sense of liberty was admitted by 7 percent of respondents.

As these results illustrate, the majority of Russians identified anxiety and other negative feelings as elements of their predominant state of mood. Russian people, according to the surveys, also tended to describe themselves in a more pessimistic, rather than optimistic way. The respondents were more likely to attribute such feelings as fear, dismay, despair, weariness, and indifference to other people than to themselves. On the contrary, feelings such as hope, self-respect, and confidence in tomorrow were more often reported as experienced by the respondents themselves, than by other people. On many measured issues, there was a gap between people's assessments of own mood and suggestions about other people's state of mind: people tended to see themselves as better off and less frustrated, anxious, or pessimistic than others (Levada, 1999a, c).

Overall, data collected by VTsIOM suggest that the level of anxiety and fears in 1999 went slightly down in comparison with 1996 surveys. In

1996, approximately one-third of respondents were interviewed just before the beginning of the presidential campaign, another third was polled between the first and second rounds, in May and June, and the remaining group was surveyed later in the summer after the end of the presidential elections. One of the reasons for such a change was perhaps linked to some changes that were taking place in Russian economy and social life during a short tenure of Prime Minister Evgeny Primakov.

Primakov relied on a small, hardworking group of professionals from intelligence and military circles who did not participate in the "privatization orgy" of the early 1990s and were free of corruption accusations. Primakov quickly reached several gentleman's agreements with key opposition factions in the Duma, including the largest and most vocal—the Communist faction. Despite a devastating financial shock of August 1998, a complete collapse of the economy predicted by many experts and the media has not taken place. These and some other factors increased Primakov's popularity, which went up to 64 percent (VTsIOM, April 9–13) and inevitable reduced fears and worries among a substantial proportion of Russians. Many Russians still based their hopes and expectations on a strong central government and "a few good men" who represented it.

Demographic Factors and Fears

Data collected in surveys by the Institute of Sociology of Russian Academy of Science in 1996 and 1999 also revealed the existence of a gender gap in assessment of anxiety and fears. The simplest division of respondents according to their sex revealed it: 70 percent of answers demonstrated differences between men and women. Results of 1996 VTsIOM surveys show that, in general, answering survey questions, Russian women tended to express greater anxiety and fears than did men. For instance, fear of unemployment was greater in women than it was in men. However, assessments of fears and concerns about issues such as social instability, decreased standards of living, crime in society, and ecological problems evoked practically similar responses from both sexes.

There was an age gap in responses regarding people's concerns about individual safety, health problems, and employment. Predictably, older age cohorts expressed greater fears than the younger respondents. This was due, perhaps, to the fact that older groups, compared to younger ones, had fewer opportunities to cope successfully with the rapidly changing societal conditions in the 1990s. The gap also existed among three basic age cohorts: youth, middle-aged, and retirees. In particular, the cohort of 49–59 year-olds reported the most intense worries than all other age groups. One possible explanation of this fact is that the retirees in Russia already had a guaranteed minimum of social protection—they secured their pensions assured by the government—whereas middle-age and pre-retirement Russians found themselves among the least adjusted to social transition as a social group.

An educational gap was also emerging from the surveys. People with more advanced college degrees tended to express greater concerns and worries about dangers such as ecological catastrophes and mass epidemics than people with less education. The more educated also expressed greater concerns about the proliferation of Western culture, "Americanization" of life, and increased influence on Russian society of non-Orthodox Christian religions, such as Islam. People of lower educational levels, on the other hand, expressed greater fears concerning impoverishment and unemployment. Expectedly, confidence in the future was higher among more educated individuals. These groups, however, as a rule, earned more money than groups with lower educational degrees and this may contribute to the differences revealed by the surveys in people's economic worries.

Overall, with some exceptions, as VTsIOM surveys (1998–2000) show, fears tend to be greater among women compared to men, older age cohorts compared to younger ones, and people with lower income and education compared to the more educated and financially secure. The only differences not statistically significant were between high school and college graduates (evaluations of hope) and between high school graduates and the less educated (evaluations of fears). (See table 2.2.)

Self-assessments of individuals' various emotional states tend to be misleading, however. Due to psychological errors in self-attribution and description of own behavior, people often tend to misjudge their own feelings (Kelley, 1967). Moreover, cultural norms of self-assessment have an

Table 2.2 "What Are the Feelings that Emerged in You Personally for the Last Years?" Source: Homo Sovieticus—III Project, 1999.

	Hope	*Fear*
Total	38	18
Men	33	10
Women	42	25
Younger than 40	33	13
Older than 40	43	23
College educated	32	13
High school educated	35	18
Less than high school	44	20

impact on people's answers to survey questions. As noted by Basina (1998, 91), "the emotional state of being offended is the state experienced by virtually all Russian citizens, regardless of their actual state of affairs, because complaining is one of the main forms of verbal self-expression." This does not mean, of course, that Russian respondents were not forthright in their judgments. The majority of Russian citizens genuinely believed that they belonged to the worst part of society. At the same time, in contradiction to the previous attitude, only a few of those who saw themselves as outsiders actually believed that the majority of Russian citizens live better than they do.

Let us now examine specific—related to particular issues and situations—concerns and fears of Russian people.

Economy and Well-Being

Polls taken in the early 1990s demonstrated a stable tendency in people's responses. About one-half of all Russians said that the dissolution of the Soviet Union was the cause of the country's economic problems; stable majorities also believed that the government and the mafia should also share the blame for the country's economy (Ratnasabapathy, 1994). Stability was one of the Russian people's principal concerns. A 1999 survey taken by VTsIOM showed that when asked what Russia's priority in the next 5 to 10 years should be—to achieve social and economic stability, or to resurrect Russia as a great power—73 percent of those polled opted for stability (The St. Petersburg Times, 1999, May 14.)

The individual's fears about economic security in the future typically reflect his or her experience and perception of current events. Events in Russia did not fuel much optimism in people's hearts. Their worries about financial safety, as well as job and social security remained high throughout the 1990s. The overall situation was such that it was hardly reasonable for an observer to expect Russian people to express more optimistic beliefs about their present and future. As an illustration, between 1990 and 1997, the Russian GDP dropped by nearly 50 percent (GKSR, 1997). By the beginning of the new millennium, the economy did not show any reliable signs of steady improvement. A relative financial stability was achieved partly because of increased cash flow due to high prices on crude oil. Meanwhile, The World Bank estimated the Russian GNP per capita in 1996 at $4,500, comparable to Egypt's $4,200 and behind developing countries, such as Colombia ($6,000) and Thailand ($8,800) (The World Bank, 1997).

Financial crises of the late 1990s did not resemble the ones that were happening in some industrial nations in South East Asia such as Korea,

Singapore, and Japan. The principal difference between Russia and those nations was that most Russians did not have monetary savings at all. For instance, in a 1994 survey by The Public Opinion Foundation, 67 percent of Russians said they did not have any savings or extra cash. For this reason, most Russians did not worry about protecting their savings from inflation (ITAR-TASS, July 29, 1994). However, the consequences of the crisis were obvious. The August 1998 financial crisis had a major sobering effect on Russian economy and entire society: Virtually everyone lost approximately three-quarters of their monthly wages. Millions of people who had savings saw them disappear from their bank accounts for the second time since 1991. In just a matter of a few days, accounts were frozen, assets turned into non-exchangeable rubles, and then gone.

During the transition period, social inequality in the nation grew. Although the estimated number of the poor in Russia varied, the State Duma assessed their total in 1999 at 34 million—an amount 14 times higher than it was in 1990. For many people, this crisis became a turning point after which cautious optimism about the future was replaced by worries about personal economic situation. Even long before the crisis, in 1997, Russian Center for Public Opinion Studies (VTsIOM) conducted a poll, which showed that only 14 percent of Russians were satisfied with their income, and 85 percent were dissatisfied.[1]

Other VTsIOM polls (1996 and 1999) show that overall, fears of impoverishment and unemployment were expressed by two thirds or greater proportions of respondents.[2] According to a survey conducted by the All-Russia Research Institute of the Russian Federation Ministry of Internal Affairs in 1997, the top spot in a ranking of fears was held by fear of losing one's job. It is experienced by 40 percent of survey respondents (Shvarov, 1997). As it follows from comparative surveys conducted in the 1990s (VTsIOM), fear of unemployment was reported by a greater number of respondents in 1999, compared to 1994. The same trend was present in surveys conducted during the same period in Poland and the Czech republic.

Anyone who had a chance to compare Russian food stores in the 1980s and 1990s (and later), would agree that the difference was striking. Although there was no abundance created in society, nevertheless, from the mid-1990s, Russians worried about hunger and famine less than they did ten years prior. According to a 1999 survey by the Public Opinion Foundation, for example, the overwhelming majority of inhabitants of Moscow and St. Petersburg did not worry about a possible famine (only 5 percent said they did). However, fears of a famine were more salient in rural areas than in cities and big towns. More than one third of rural residents by the end of the 1990s feared food shortages and possible starvation (*Ekonomika i Zhizn,* 1999, n. 39, September, p. 32).

Other Concerns: Crime and Environment

It was argued by Alexander Golov (*Monitoring of Public Opinion, 1995,* no *3.*) that the sources of tensions in Russian society are mostly social and that the sources of satisfactions and joys are mostly personal. According to 1999 *Homo Sovieticus* project data, the most widespread objects of fear were: unemployment (85 percent), authorities' arbitrariness (76 percent) and criminals' attacks (74 percent). At the same time, the utmost satisfaction and joy people reported to receive: from children (35 percent), "great money" (33 percent), and [owning private] gardens (28 percent).

In a 1999 survey of five Russian regions, the majority of respondents expressed "constant fear" (the strongest indicator on the answer scale) and "strong anxiety" (second on the scale) about a wide variety of issues and problems. Although the number of people who expressed their anxiety slightly decreased, compared to a 1996 survey, a minimum of four in ten Russians still expressed their "constant" fears about a variety of specific problems. According to this survey, people's responses did not significantly differ from region to region. Thus, "complete lawlessness" as a source of constant fear and anxiety was mentioned by 61 percent of Moscow and St. Petersburg residents (the biggest and most advanced economically Russian cities) and by 60 and 59 percent of residents of Russian South and Southwest and North and Northwest regions respectively. From 60 to 68 percent of residents in five Russian regions mentioned crime as a main source of their concerns. There are only small cross-regional differences revealed by the survey. More than two thirds of residents of Volga River and the Urals districts (69 percent) expressed their fear about mass epidemics. In other regions, no more than 55 percent (and no less than 48 percent) of respondents expressed this fear.

Two national surveys administered by VTsIOM in 1994 and 1999 also showed insignificant differences in people's expressions of their anxiety and fear. Respondents were asked to assign the intensity of their fear on a 5-point scale from (1) "no fear at all" to (5) "constant fear." There were no significant differences in people's responses except one: As was mentioned earlier, in 1999, fear of unemployment was reported as more significant than it was in 1994 (people in 1999 assessed their fear of unemployment as 4.1 points of the scale, compared to 3.5 points in 1994). In both surveys, the strongest concern was expressed about "maladies of the loved ones" (4.3 and 4.5 points in 1994 and 1999 surveys respectively). Issues such as "world war" (received 3.6 points in both surveys) and "criminal attacks" (3.9 and 3.6) were the sources of less concern. Among the least significant sources of worries mentioned were "natural calamities" (3.1 points in both surveys), "return to mass repressions" (3.2 and 2.9), and "ethnic violence" (3.4 and 3.3).

Maladies of the loved ones were identified as the prime object of fears, ranked number one in overall "lists" of people's worries. This should not be surprising because concerns about relatives and closest friends are typically among the most common human worries. One of the "maladies" mentioned in surveys is poor quality of the individual's health and health-care services in post-Soviet Russia. More than one in every third Russian acknowledged that he or she experienced concerns about the possibility of losing one's family member due to illness or accident (35 percent of respondents). Many people feared their "own maladies" as well. According to another survey, about 30 percent of the surveyed acknowledged their worries about contracting an incurable disease (Shvarov, 1997).

Such fears ought to be deemed reasonable. One of the major societal indicators—life expectancy—dropped from 67 years in 1994 to 57 years for men, and from 76 to 70 for women. From 1992 to 1997, the death rate in Russia was so high that 4 million more people died than were born. Moreover, the birth rate continuously decreased. By the end of the 1990s, there were 3.7 million fewer children in Russia than there were in 1990. The number of suicides in the country was twice that of late 1980s, and reached the 60,000-per-year mark. For one of every 100 live births in Russia, there were 180 abortions performed (all data from Russian State Duma, 1999). Many diseases that almost vanished during the Soviet years, such as tuberculosis and diphtheria, were back on a massive scale (Malashenko, 1999, October). The overall population of the country decreased by several million, despite the influx of over 4 million refugees from other areas of the former Soviet Union. The 1990s was a period of the worst depopulation of Russia since World War II (Ryurikov, 1999).

Crime was also a serious source of concerns in the 1990s. In a survey administered in 1997 and reported by *Nezavisimaya Gazeta* (Shvarov, 1997), 27 percent of Russians were afraid of being severely injured or killed at the hands of criminals, and 26 percent feared becoming victims of thieves and thugs. The overall crime level in the country caused anxiety among 38 percent of survey respondents, 50 percent said they were seriously concerned about it, and only 12 percent did not worry about it at all. According to the same study, people's worry about crime was partly due to a low level of trust in law enforcement agencies: 60 percent of the survey respondents reported a lack of confidence in law officers' ability to give them the competent assistance they need. Moreover, 38 percent of survey respondents wanted to possess firearms, and the main reason for this is they were seeking ways to protect themselves from criminals.

One of the remarkable attitudinal trends of the 1990s was a decline in the extent of people's concerns about environmental problems, which became less salient in people's opinions. The importance of environmental problems was partially shadowed by problems such as impoverishment, unemployment, and crime. In 1999, 52 percent of Russians expressed their concerns about "chemical and radiating poison of water, air, and [food] products," which was a 16-point drop from a survey that asked the same question in 1996. Nevertheless, ten years after the world's worst nuclear plant accident in Chernobyl, many Russians expressed concerns that a nuclear accident could happen again. (See chapters on Belarus and Ukraine in this book). Although a slim majority of Muscovites surveyed by Mnenie public opinion service in 1996 were not sure about their fear or said nuclear disasters were unlikely, Russia's seven aging nuclear plants with 29 Soviet-made reactors in them are perceived as a threat by many of the surveyed. In this poll, nearly 45 percent of respondents reported they still feared a similar catastrophe could happen in Russia (AP, 1996). A national poll conducted four years later, in 2000, by VTsIOM showed that 26 percent of Russians considered the possibility of an accident similar to what happened at the Chernobyl nuclear power plant in Ukraine "very likely." Another 43 percent regarded such a possibility as "rather likely," and 21 percent as either "unlikely" or "impossible" (Interfax, 2000, April 24).

At the end of the 1980s, when government's censorship of the mass media was weakening, journalists faced little control over what natural disasters and accidents they could cover in their reports. Even though in the 1990s television news and newspaper publications were filled with information about disasters and accidents, there were no tremendous hikes of fear of natural calamities among Russian people.

Assessments of Foreign Threats

Individuals who experience frustration may establish identifiable objects against which they could vent their irritation. On the societal level, such dissatisfaction can be "redirected" and projected onto some domestic and external targets—individuals, social groups, and entire countries. Such a process of "enemy-searching" was taking place in Germany in the late 1920s and 1930s. Some experts suggested that Russia was set to repeat this gruesome experience of so-called Weimar Syndrome (Rozov, 1997). One such target of frustration could become Western countries, the apparent victors in the Cold War. Ex-foreign minister Kozyrev (1995) declared confidently, referring to the average individual, that Russians do not have anti-Western instincts. However, this opinion was correct only to some extent. Popular psychological frustrations, in fact, grew in a sizable proportion of Russian individuals with consistently negative feelings toward the West and the United States (Shiraev and Zubok, 2001).

The late 1980s and early 1990s were marked by people's optimistic beliefs in the almost unlimited opportunities of bilateral Russian-American and international cooperation. Such beliefs began to evaporate and morph into more pessimistic and frustration-driven isolationistic attitudes among many Russian people (Interfax 1995, 21 September). This trend, however, did not mean that many Russians sought to quarrel with the United States. Very few people believed in the high probability of a major war between Russia and America (Kelley 1994). At the same time, almost one third of Russians named the United States as a potential aggressor against Russia (Smirnov, 1997). Although individual fears about possible wars were contingent on immediate international developments—such as the NATO eastward expansion and especially the war in Kosovo in 1999—the Cold War "enemy image" was returning.

The threat of aggression from a foreign country was expressed by 12 percent of respondents in a 1999 survey by the Public Opinion Foundation (*Ekonomika i Zhizn,* 1999, n. 39, September, p. 32). According to other polls by the Public Opinion Foundation (summer 1999 and spring 1999), the NATO enlargement to the east was a threat to Russia according to 66 and 51 percent of respondents respectively. In an August 1999 poll by the Public Opinion Foundation, people were asked a question, "What country do you think is a source of a nuclear war threat?" Most respondents—44 percent—identified the United States as the number one nuclear threat. Most Russians did not include countries such as Iraq, China, and Iran into the category of nuclear threats: Iraq was mentioned by 14 percent, Iran was referred to in 11 percent of responses, and China was named by 10 percent of respondents. More than one in every fourth Russian did not know what country to pick and 5 percent suggested the country did not face any nuclear threat from the outside.

In 1996, 67 percent of Russians were afraid of the accession of the Baltic sovereign countries Latvia, Estonia, and Lithuania to NATO. This move, in these people's view, would pose a threat to Russia's security, as it was shown by a poll conducted in 1996 by the Moscow-based Center for International Sociological Research. From the Russian perspective, NATO has done little to dispel its Cold-War image. Most Russians did not understand why NATO forces should be introduced into countries from which Russia has removed its troops. They will consider the expansion of NATO an overt threat to Russia's national security. At the same time, there were indications that people's concern was not NATO itself but its overall attitude toward Russia. In fact, in the mid-1990s, Russians tended to support the idea that their country would join NATO, even though for decades many Russians regarded the Western military alliance as the prime foe of the Soviet Union, the poll showed. Russia's accession to NATO had the support of 75 percent of those polled, with 20 percent against and 5 percent having no opinion (*Baltic News Service,* 1996, January 15).

Muscovites maintained more pro-Western attitudes than the rest of the country. Most residents did not turn their backs on the West and the United States (Shiraev 1999). For example, in a 1997 survey by the Mnenie Polling Service, less than 25 percent of Muscovites considered NATO an enemy. Nationwide opinion polls on the same subject showed more negative feelings against NATO prevailed in other Russian regions (MacWilliam 1997). Specifically, 32 percent of Muscovites did not rule out the possibility that NATO military forces might interfere in the settlement of local conflicts in Russia, for example, the war in Chechnya, says an opinion poll conducted by the All-Russian Fund for Public Opinion Studies in May 1999. The poll involved about 1,000 respondents. However, 56 percent of those polled did not believe that such interference was possible (Interfax, May 14, 1999). However, it was not clear whether the respondents liked the idea of American involvement. It is likely that they did not. Results of various polls taken by VTsIOM in the 1990s show a stable pattern of negative attitudes toward the United States and the West: one quarter to one third of respondents express these opinions. Even prospects of cooperation with the United States were rejected by many individuals: According to Public Opinion Foundation (September 23, 1999), 22 percent of Russians considered cooperation with the United States and other Western countries harmful to Russia.

Fear of Terrorism

Political and social developments can produce new kinds of popular worries and fears. One such "new" fear—which became familiar to many Russians in the end of the 1990s—was fear of terrorist attacks against civilian population. In accordance with a 1999 survey conducted by the All-Russian Center of Public Opinion Research, long before the tragic events in the United States, 88 percent of Russians were afraid of being victims of a terrorist act (*Novoe Vremya,* no 40, October 1999, p. 9.) The Chechen war, which continued throughout the 1990s and later, was the prime contributor to these fears. The solid consequences of the Yeltsin regime's inability to solve the Chechen problem, these fears at one point became a source of consolidation of public opinion to support Vladimir Putin and the new leadership in the summer of 1999.

We cannot help but agree that political leaders threatening their voters with apocalyptic forecasts are socially irresponsible, but this sort of behavior is rational in that it adequately responds to the non-verbal wishes and demands of the public. The proliferation of mass fears after the devastating explosions in Moscow and other cities of Russia (August and September 1999) have played an important role in triggering a substantial support of those who advocated the tougher line against Chechen separatists. Contrary to the polls conducted during different periods of escalation of the Chechen war, most people expressed their support of the campaign. In October and December 1999, according to VTsIOM, more than 50 percent of respondents indicated that "anxiety" characterized their emotion when dealing with information on Russia's military actions in Chechnya; less than 25 percent viewed these actions with "satisfaction" and less than 10 percent mentioned "shame."

Even though no person was officially charged as the result of the 1999 Moscow explosions, public opinion announced its verdict promptly: 76 percent of people put their blames on Chechen militants. More than 39 percent of Russians feared that the separatists impose danger to Russia's sovereignty and 60 percent reported they feared terrorists (Kertman, 2000.)

On September 12 and 13 (2001), right after the terrorist attacks on the United States, VTsIOM conducted a poll of 400 Moscow residents. The terrorist attacks primarily aroused indignation in 52 percent of respondents. In Moscow, 28 percent of respondents mentioned feeling fear. In Moscow, 50 percent of respondents considered other terrorist attacks possible in other countries. Along with this, 41 percent said that the September 2001 terrorist attacks might lead to beginning of a new world war.

Attempting to measure people's concerns related to a potential escalation of the United States' military campaign in Afghanistan, the Public Opinion Foundation conducted a poll of 1,500 city and town residents on October 13, 2001. Sixty-four per cent of those polled said that the U.S. military operation in Afghanistan was dangerous for Russia. Thirty-six per cent said they feared Russia's involvement in a local or global military conflict. Five percent of those polled said they feared that Russia might be attacked by international terrorists if it supported the United States.

Overall, No Fear of Social Backlash

As it was mentioned earlier in this chapter, Russians answering questions in opinion polls tended to distinguish between their own, local situation, and their perception of what was going on in the country. For instance, according to a May 1999 VTsIOM survey, the economic situation in people's towns or districts was viewed as good or satisfactory by 24 percent of those surveyed; 52 percent indicated it was bad; "very bad" suggested 16 percent. However, the economic situation in the country was viewed as good or satisfactory by 11 percent, bad by 49 percent, and very bad by 34 percent (*Monitoring,* 1999.) According to polls conducted by the Public

Opinion Foundation at the same time, 54 percent of Russians anticipated "mass rallies and protest actions" in the country, while only 34 percent expected them in their own regions. To some extent, fears of social calamities grew from distrust in the federal authorities whose policies, in opinion of most Russians, completely determined the situation in the country (Public Opinion Foundation, 1999).

According to a comparative study co-sponsored by the USIA, 63 percent of individuals in Russia in the early 1990s said the most pronounced threat to them was coming from potential unrest within their own country (Weber, 1992). The threat of fascism in Russia was real, according to 57 percent of respondents in St. Petersburg and Moscow. However, there was a noticeable disagreement in opinions about sources of Russian fascism. Educated people and those who belonged to younger age cohorts considered fascism as advocated by the poor, whereas the poor tended to believe that fascism was supported by the wealthy (Kondratenko, 1995).

Were Russians afraid of dictatorship? A possibility of dictatorship and mass repressions in Russia worried only 6 percent of people, according to the Public Opinion Foundation (*Ekonomika i Zhizn,* 1999, n. 39, September, p. 32.) This result can be interpreted from at least two points of view. On one hand, it seems to be that very few people were really concerned about an "iron fist" in Kremlin because they believed that democratic institutions in Russia were strong enough to sustain a threat of authoritarianism. On the other hand, dictatorship could have been perceived as a desirable turn of events because many people would support tough measures aimed at bringing the country back to a state of order and stability. In this case, in some people's view, "mass repressions" could have targeted those who were responsible for the country's problems, such as, criminals, corrupt officials, and "traitors" of all kinds.[3]

Fears of authoritarianism grew, nevertheless, in 1999. According to a VTsIOM poll taken in September 2000 (national sample), a sizable 38 percent of people feared the advent of authoritarian regime in Russia: They said dictatorship could happen definitely or was most likely. Even though 50 percent of respondents said that they did not fear dictatorship, most people still worried about anarchy, chaos, and collapse of the country: 60 percent confirmed the existence of this fear, with 33 percent replying they did not have it (Golovachev, 2000). People's anticipation of riots and social unrest significantly relaxed with the appointment and then election of President Putin. On the eve of the presidential elections in March 2000, only 16 percent expected an increase in mass rallies and protests, while 17 percent believed such actions would subside. Others suggested no significant changes. A year earlier, in March 1999, the opinion about an increase in mass protests was voiced by 54 percent, with only 5 percent expressing disagreement (POR, 2000).

Overall, warnings about the dangers of a communist, fascist, nationalistic, or any other type of backlash did not become reality in Russia. Unlike Germany before World War II, Russia did not have necessary social and political conditions that might have caused landslide violence (Devlin, 1999.)

Conclusion

A popular expression among Russians of the 1990s was: "We are not living, we are surviving." The difference between the verbs "to live" and "to survive" is not only semantic. It stands for a tremendous gap between people's wishes and reality, between expectations and hopes, on one hand, and gloomy outcomes of the societal transformation on the other. The "surviving" Russian individual is a special kind of a person. He or she has to develop a specific set of personal traits and features. In the repertoire of these traits, anything is appropriate that helps the individual to continue to exist. On one hand, people have to learn how to rely on themselves and scrape by until better days arrive. Becoming adaptive under harsh conditions, such survival traits may reduce the individual's fears: If expectations are low, there is no reason to worry much about the dangers and tribulations of your life.

On the other hand, the "surviving" Russian individual becomes increasingly dependent on the authorities. In fact, despite many social transitions taking place in post-Soviet Russia, authorities are still very much responsible for practically every element of people's lives—from establishing laws that significantly affect people's daily activities, such as making decisions about distributing apartments, hot water rationing, changing bus routes, or building health care clinics to paying salaries and pensions to the majority of Russians. Such reliance on somebody else's power can develop a sense of dependency and reduce people's aspirations. In addition, beliefs that the majority of Russian people are poor and without rights may reinforce the feeling of pessimism and beliefs that only benevolent but tough authorities can correct the situation (Kertman, 2000). Belief in the all-powerful authorities prompts Russians to think that the country's future depends on the personal and professional qualities of the people at the top of the pyramid of power—the president and the prime minister.

It is difficult to measure the direct impact of Russian political rhetoric—typically conveyed via the media—among high-ranked politicians and officials on the fears and worries of Russian people. However, the knowledgeable observer may notice that throughout the 1990s, most

Russian political leaders, including the moderates, preferred to debate their opponents using an "apocalyptic" language, arguing that the opponents' policies would inevitably lead to economic disaster, civil war, and complete social disintegration. Some people, no doubt, were frightened by this rhetoric. Others grew accustomed to this gloom-and-doom language. It is quite obvious that there are many Russians who do not believe that their country is in a disastrous state, and they do not necessarily feel anxiety, dismay, and fear for their future.

Notes

1. Favorable perception of political and social events may affect the level of worries and anxiety in people, a change that can become noticeable in polls. For example, right after Yevgeny Primakov was appointed prime minister, the number of respondents expecting increased social tensions dropped by more than one third. There was a nine-point increase in people's assessments of their economic situation. After Putin was appointed prime minister, improvement of the country's economic situation in 2000 was anticipated by 39 percent, a 25-point hike from the same period of 1998.
2. There were differences in expression of fears about poverty and unemployment in various Russian regions. For example, in 1999, respondents from the Volga River and the Urals district expressed greater concerns about these issues (81 and 74 percent of people respectively) than did people in other regions. The gap was within 11–20 percentage points.
3. President Putin early days' popular and actively promoted motto was "dictatorship of the law." The reaction to this slogan was generally mixed and based on where, in the observer's eye, the emphasis was: was it on the word "dictatorship" or on "the law"?

Chapter 3

The Czech Republic: Transitional Worries

Martina Klicperová-Baker

In December 1996, when the Czech president Václav Havel underwent a serious operation and was bedded down in an intensive care unit, millions of Czechs were worried about his life but very few feared for the future of their country: Ten million citizens of the Czech Republic had already lived in a democratic society that underwent dramatic transformations and was quite different from the country and society prior to the Velvet Revolution of 1989. Freedom and democracy were restored, the Soviet and communist domination ceased to exist. A comeback of the Communist Party to political power that followed in many European transitional societies did not materialize. Most people were confident in their country's democratic traditions and their continuity. Many international critics and experts were talking about the "Czech model" of transition, emphasizing its positive features and advantages.

Under these apparently favorable conditions, what types of fears and concerns did people in this European country develop? Did everything go "smoothly" so that people were free of fears and worries? The post-revolutionary decade was not homogenous and smooth. At least three distinct periods in this decade can be identified.

The Early Post-Revolutionary Years: Euphoria

The Czech society was enjoying a state of euphoria stemming from the peaceful transition from communist authoritarianism to a free and democratic state. The first true multi-party elections had a massive turnout. Former communists were barred from public offices by the "lustration law." The Czechs adored their new president, Havel, and supported the new cabinet of Prime Minister Václav Klaus. Although prices went up as a result of their deregulation, it did not cause severe consequences: People were prepared to sustain some difficulties. The dramatic increase of crime rate was perceived as a temporary and inevitable tax for freedom."

The most serious problem that Czechoslovakia faced was the sustainability of the country's federation. Until the end of 1992, the Czech lands constituted the dominant part of the multinational Czechoslovak Federal Republic, where Czechs, Moravians, and Silesians were sharing political power with Slovaks. The Slovak demands for sovereignty met Czech willingness to negotiate. Czechs and Slovaks did not wage a war against each other, and hostility never materialized between the groups while the two nations negotiated a rational, peaceful split. The Czech foreign policy followed a popular doctrine, "back to Europe," with a hope for early inclusion to European and world democratic structures. The Czechs were proud to be considered the model nation in transition to democracy.

The Second Half of the 1990s: Growing Disenchantment

People's opinions about the course of events in their country were changing during the 1990s. Although throughout the 90s a sizable proportion of respondents (from 30 to 47 percent) viewed the preceding year as "both good and bad," satisfaction and confidence were more common for 1990 and the mid-1990s compared to the end of the decade. Concurrently, disappointment grew. In 1990, for instance, 45 percent of people evaluated the previous year as "good" and 19 percent as "bad." In 1999, only 9 percent evaluated the previous year as "good," whereas 42 percent said it was "bad" (IVVM, Rezková 2000c).

The Czech government in the early period has gained a substantial political capital due to the peaceful split with Slovakia and prospects of an early inclusion to NATO. Nevertheless, continuing economic decline, price hikes, and unemployment began to threaten a growing number of people. In particular, the fact that the state started to repeal innumerable subsidies and benefits from various areas was traumatizing to those who were raised under the communist regime. While people were ready for the initial shock therapy in the early 1990s, most of them were not prepared for the continuing economic decline. Some government officials turned out to be equally prone to corruption as the communist administrators from the previous regime. Prime Minister Klaus resigned after accusations of illegal financial deals.

Ten Years after the Revolution: Onset of Realistic Corrections

Economic and political difficulties did not cause mass alienation and indifference among most Czechs. On the contrary, the curtailing of pluralistic freedom by the actions of two leading political parties (so-called "Opposition Agreement") triggered popular dissatisfaction and even mass protests. Those faithful to the ideals of the Velvet Revolution protested in the streets at the occasion of its 10th anniversary and again in early 2001, defending independence of the public television. People came to the realization that political transition is a long and difficult process, which requires civic alertness and skills as well as persistence.

Post-Totalitarian Syndrome vs. the Democratic Anchor

To make sense of what worried people in the Czech Republic most during the societal transition, let us get back to the late 1980s. Most European communist regimes in their final, Thermidorean phase were increasingly populist in attempts to secure loyalty from citizens and keep the masses from challenging the system (Feierabend et al., 1999). Czechoslovak government of that period made a deliberate and persistent effort to persuade people about the importance of the benefits of socialism, such as entitlement to welfare, free education, and universal health coverage—all guaranteed by the Communist Party. Despite shortages and low salaries (the average was about $200 a month), most of the population in Czechoslovakia under the communist regime enjoyed inexpensive housing with $5–10 monthly rents, subsidized groceries (a bread roll for a cent, two pounds of apples for a nickel, mug of beer for a dime), transportation (a bus ticket for 3 cents), and even cultural events (books and opera tickets for a dollar). The government, suppressing basic human liberties, was able to curb street crime and provide for the individual's basic needs. Overall, failing in the ideological arena, the government turned to the principles of so-called *goulash communism:* emphasizing welfare benefits and granting privileges to those who were willing to collaborate with their regime.

This dependency on the paternalistic authority together with individual irresponsibility constitutes the main symptom of what might be called the post-communist syndrome. Other symptoms of this syndrome include: learned helplessness, intolerance, stereotypical thinking, external locus of control, distrust, conformity, broken ties with neighborhood and community, and the lack of civic virtues.[1]

To comprehend what worried (or did not worry) people in the Czech Republic during the societal transition, one has to look back beyond the communist times into the era of the first Czechoslovak republic (1918–1938) and its glory as preserved in historical documents and people's memories. The notion that these years of democratic Czechoslovakia belong to the best times of the modern Czech history is deeply embedded even in the young Czech generations. Therefore, if we try to understand the level and type of transitional worries in the Czechs, it is necessary to realize that for many people of this nation transition to democracy was not a step into the unknown. Quite the opposite, it was very clearly defined as a return, a homecoming to the good old days. The slogan "back to Europe" (which was implying a release from the "Asiatic," i.e., Soviet communism) became very popular. It was argued that the social changes in Czechoslovakia should be discussed in terms of *transition* (i.e., transfer from one known state to the other, restoration of continuity) rather than *transformation* (continuing change without defined goals) (Klicperová-Baker, 1999).

Judging their lives in retrospective, ten years after the democratic revolution 68 percent of Czechs said that the events of November 17, 1989 had brought fundamental changes to their lives (CTK, 1999, November 17). Whether the Czech Velvet Revolution is considered a real revolution or *refolution* (a blend of *ref*orm and rev*olution*), a substantial political change of the governing regime and society in general was accomplished. The leaders of the revolution followed through with their promise of a peaceful change. Therefore, fears of retaliation and threats of bloodshed (which both had been the case after the defeat of the Nazis in 1945) were absent.

Quality of Life: Basic Worries

Overall, the economic changes that took place in the Czech society in the 1990s were inevitably associated with the demise of the paternalistic welfare system. During the first years of transition, there was a great effort undertaken by the government to explain the meaning of the planned socioeconomic policies to the citizens. That largely prevented the appearance of irrational fears and helped the people to cope with the changes successfully. On January 1, 1991, the process of privatization officially started, which sparked legitimate worries about inflation. Even though as early as in the late 1980s the signs of inflation were obvious,[2] due to the well-planned educational campaign, fears of a monetary catastrophe never prevailed: Most of the population was in anticipation of a major improvement in their lives and willing to withstand the initial shock. Most of eligible citizens registered for the voucher privatization campaign and studied the basics of investing. Life suddenly provided a host of new opportunities.

The reintroduction of free market to the Czech society did not only mean opportunities in a new competitive environment (e.g., opportunity of picking good stock in voucher privatization or starting one's own business) but also a possibility to lose. In the first place, there was a loss of a very predictable environment. However, the challenge did not seem to exceed the coping ability of most citizens. The Czechs almost habitually complain, and a little bit of grumble is almost as much a component of a Czech friendly greeting as "I am fine" is a constituent of American conversation. Perhaps it is a residual part of survival skills from the times when one had to keep a low profile and being problem-free was suggestive of collaboration with the disdained oppressive regimes; it may also be a routine to prevent envy of less fortune fellows. Yet, when polled about their fears or worries, a substantial part of Czech respondents could not report any that would trouble them (see the first line of table 3. 1).

The process of change affected the individual's feeling of security, stability, and a predictable future. Under the new social and political conditions, satisfaction of numerous basic human needs (Maslow, 1970) required significant effort, skills, and individual responsibility—the features that many people were lacking at that time. As a result, disappointment and fears grew among those social groups that generally failed to adjust to the ongoing changes.

Table 3.1 Personal Fears and Worries of People in the Czech Republic in 1997–2000, Percentage of Positive Answers (IVVM—Rezková, 2000a)

When you think of your current situation, what worries you the most? Are you afraid of something? If yes, what is it? (Single response)	*1997*	*1998*	*1999*	*2000*
No worries	31	26	23	30
Financial problems	23	30	17	12
Worries related to a job, studies	12	14	25	27
Health	16	10	15	14
Worsening of political situation	5	9	3	2
Economic problems of the country	< 2	5	5	4
General insecurity about future	3	3	4	3
Growth of crime, safety fears	3	< 2	2	3
War conflicts	< 2	< 2	3	2
Other responses (also include < 2 responses from above)	5	3	3	3

Many competent individuals did not feel threatened by the changes; instead, they appreciated a chance to satisfy their needs of growth. These people typically cherished freedom and supported democratization. Liberation also freed citizens from fear of state terror and humiliation of their individuality. Nevertheless, it triggered many other significant fears related to personal safety and survival. Passive and unwilling, many individuals incapable of change felt threatened by the ongoing transition and feared that they would not be able to satisfy their basic needs.

People identified diverse dangers to democracy and various sources of their worries. Some 15 percent of Czechs viewed "old structures" (communism and the Communist Party) as the greatest dangers to democracy, while 11 percent regarded economic problems, unemployment, and bank collapses to be the greatest dangers. Some 9 percent of respondents viewed corruption and economic crime as the biggest threats to democracy, and the same percentage said the biggest threats to democracy were political conflicts and political instability. Nine percent stated that democracy is threatened by negative attitudes, jealousy and fanaticism. Only one percent meant that there was no danger to democracy at all (CTK, 2000, August 11, 2000).

Most people in a country going through a period of economic and social transition have to deal with an uneasy predicament: The new economic system that is supposed to bring prosperity and stability to people's lives is based on free competition. The state no longer guarantees and provides for a certain level of living standards available to everyone. For years Czechs lived in a socialist country, in which they were entitled to what they called *jistoty* (social guarantees), a comprehensive set of economic benefits, the distribution of which was monitored by the state. As in other socialist societies, Czech citizens had guaranteed salaries, health care, pensions, subsidized housing, energy, and public transportation. One of the main sources of anxiety and worries for most people during the transition period in the Czech Republic was not the threat of starvation or devastating poverty but learning what the real market value of things and services was and figuring out which social benefits would be "guaranteed" by the state and which would not. Frustration and worries stemmed, in part, from people's realization that many benefits guaranteed to them a few years ago now must be earned. For many individuals this realization was associated with the threat of a loss of something significant: their habits, priorities, even lifestyle. Many feared lowering of the quality of their lives. For example, according to a 1992 poll of 577 Czechs and 505 Slovaks, the biggest worry of people surveyed (26 percent) was a danger of a drop in their standard of living (CTK, 1992, October 13). In 1995 and 2000, a national sample was given a list of 18 problem areas, respondents were asked which ones they considered "very urgent," "fairly urgent," "somewhat urgent" or "not urgent." Consistently, 56 and 50 percent of Czechs (in 1995 and 2000 respectively) stated that an important social issue—the health care—was a "very urgent" problem that the country faced. In both surveys, about six out of ten respondents believed that the problem of social "guarantees" (such as benefits and pensions) was also very urgent. In 2000, 76 percent of Czechs said unemployment was a "very urgent" problem, compared to 37 percent in 1995. Overall, the polls confirmed the prevailing significance of personal material worries and illustrated a gradual change in their contents: Fears of financial problems were slowly easing (people getting used to the gradual hikes in prices) being replaced by worry of joblessness (as prices started to settle, unemployment kept rising) (IVVM, Rezková, 2000a).

Concerns about losing a job appear justifiable in a country in which the unemployment rate has risen from low single digits in the early 1990s to almost 10 percent in 2000. However, a more detailed analysis provides a more refined picture of these concerns. Even though in November 1994, 34 percent of respondents reported a serious fear of unemployment, still, the majority, 66 percent, said they had little or no fear of losing job at all (CTK, 1994, November 23). Three years later, 74 percent of Czechs still reported they did not fear that they might lose their job, according to a poll conducted by IVVM (CTK, 1997, November 3). In 2000, according to a poll by the STEM polling agency, more than half of Czechs adults were afraid of losing their jobs. However, the same number of people (59 percent) were confident that if they became unemployed, they would be capable of finding another job or get training that would lead to a job change (CTK, 2000, April 22). Table 3.2 provides a snapshot of several polls taken between 1989 and 2000, which reflect some' concerns about particular economic problems associated with' transition (including fear of unemployment measured by different polling organizations). Worries about people's finances grew by 1998 (the period of an economic crisis in the country) but became less significant by 2000.

Overall, Czechs were not preoccupied with a fear that their country's economy would go bankrupt or there would be food shortages. It is quite reasonable that many (and polls show that their number reaches about one-third of the population) expressed fears about particular financial problems and dangers. In four opinion polls conducted between 1997 and 2000, people were asked to give a single response to the question: "When you think about your current situation, what worries you the most? Are you afraid of something? If yes, what is it?" During the three-year period, no more than 5 percent of respondents mentioned the country's economic

Table 3.2 A Comparison of Various Economic Fears and Worries Expressed by Czechs. Selected Polls (1989–2000).

Type of "economic" fears or concerns	*Year*	*Percent*
Fear of shortages in food supply[a]	1989	37
Fear of price increase[a]	1990	69
Concerns about economic developments in the country[b]	1993	24
Worries that within the next two years respondents would not be able to pay for housing[c]	1993	46
Concerns that privatization would bring hard times[d]	1994	40
Great fear of price increase[e]	1994	40
Great fear of unemployment[e]	1994	34
Great fear of high medical expenses[e]	1994	36
Fear of deepening economic crisis[f]	1995	15
Fear that the country is going bankrupt[g]	1996	13
Fear of increasing rent[h]	1996	28
Fear of unemployment[i]	1998	41
Fear of price increase[a]	1999	74
Fear of shortages in food supply[a]	1999	6
Fear that unemployment will increase in the next two years[j]	2000	75
Fear of losing job[k]	2000	59

[a]Poll by: The Center of Empirical Studies. Source: CTK, 1999, November 11
[b]Poll by: The Center of Empirical Studies. Source: CTK, 1993, August 19
[c]Source: CTK, 1993, August 27
[d]Poll by: the Institute of Public Opinion Research. Source: Sedlák, 1994
[e]Poll by: Public Opinion Research. Source: CTK, 1994, November 23
[f]Poll by: GFK. Source: CTK, 1995, August 8
[g]Source: CTK, 1996, May 15
[h]Poll by: the Institute of Public Opinion Research. Source: CTK, 1996, December 12
[i]Poll by: STEM. Source: CTK, 1998, September 22
[j]Poll by: the Institute for Public Opinion Research. Source: CTK, 2000, March 20
[k]Poll by: STEM. Source: CTK, 2000, April 22

problems as the source of their fears. Although personal financial problems were mentioned as most worrisome by 30 percent of people in 1998, this source of worry had lost its significance by 2000, when only 12 percent mentioned them. Altogether, the results of these polls suggest that even though a number of people had specific concerns about their money, education, or career, there was an overall trust in the country's economy, an attitude that perhaps eased many individual's fears about their future (IVVM, Rezková, 2000a).

It is quite remarkable that, contrary to most post-communist democracies (compare cases of Russia and Ukraine in this book, for example), economic problems of the Czech Republic were not on the list of the most significant concerns.

Fears about Crime

Crime causes significant concerns in most societies. Major social changes tend to bring a dramatic increase in crime and the Czech society was no exception. As mentioned in chapter 1, answers to surveys depend on the formulation of a question and the specific situation in which the poll is taken. For example, crime may not appear as a serious problem if respondents are asked what is their own personal worry (IVVM, Rezková, 2000a).[3]

Other polling showed that the majority of Czechs viewed crime as a very serious social issue (CTK, 1999, November 11). In 1995, almost half of the interviewed evaluated the overall safety situation in the country as "bad" (CTK, 1995, January 5). GfK Market Research Institute reported that 45 percent of Czechs claimed they were mostly afraid of increased crime in the country (CTK, 1995, August 8). Specifically, according to this study, 78 percent of the Czechs feared the loss of their property—most worried about burglary, theft of a car, and robbery.

Pollsters from the IVVM agency ask the Czechs annually not only about their personal fears but also about general national issues that may worry the respondents. Repeatedly, in 1995 and 2000, respondents were given a list of 18 problem areas and were asked which ones they consider "very urgent," "fairly urgent," "somewhat urgent" or "not urgent" (IVVM, Rezková, 2000a). The most distressing issues chosen from the list were "corruption" (in 1995 73 percent and in 2000 79 percent considered it "very urgent), "organized crime" (66 and 70 percent respectively) and "common crime" (76 and 62 percent).

General concerns about crime in society indeed differ from fears about crime interpreted as threats to the individual's safety. Only one-third of people surveyed in 2000 said they personally feared organized crime, economic crime, and corruption. On the other hand, almost half of citizens feared these types of crime threaten the Czech Republic as a country, according to data released by the Sofres-Factum polling agency. So, on the personal level, the most intense feeling of threat of economic crime was reported by 31 percent of the questioned, 26 percent were afraid of organized crime and 24 percent of corruption. With respect to the threat to the state, intense danger was perceived from economic crime by 50 percent of people, organized crime was seen as a menace by 40 percent respondents and 48 percent claimed that the state was threatened by corruption (CTK, 2000, April 16). Even though people expressed intense rational concerns about the general state of affairs, they attributed less anxiety to the impact of crime on their personal lives.[4]

One of the factors that stimulated criminal activities after the Velvet Revolution was the sudden opening of the country's borders. Political and social transitions allowed rapid development of the organized and international crime in Eastern Europe. The Czech Republic became an attractive place for various gangs, members of which had a convenient access to most European capitals. Smuggling, car theft, racketeering, contract killings, and fraud became almost ordinary topics for coverage by local television networks and newspapers. Russian, Yugoslav, East Asian, Bulgarian, Italian, Polish, Romanian, Albanian, Turkish and other "ethnic" criminal groups in the country started their struggle for lucrative markets and activities. Patriotic Czechs joked, "If at least these were our own, Czech mafias!"

Criminal acts committed by these gangs reinforced development of xenophobic tendencies among Czechs.

Worries about Foreigners

Waves of political changes in the last decade of the twentieth century had brought scores of migrants and asylum seekers to the Czech Republic. Immigration to the Czech lands was a relatively new social phenomenon. In preceding years, many people emigrated from Czechoslovakia, especially after the dramatic events of the communist coup of 1948 and after the 1968 Warsaw Pact invasion. After World War II, most ethnic Germans, living primarily in the border regions of Czechoslovakia, were driven back to Germany while Czech Ruthenians and their lands were seized by the Soviet Union. A sizable group of ethnic Hungarians became Slovak citizens after the Czechoslovak separation in 1992. Perhaps only ethnic Slovaks living in the Czech Republic and Roma (the Gypsies) represented distinct ethnic minority until the recent wave of immigrants reached the Czech Republic.

Similarly to many other East European countries, xenophobic attitudes were present among Czech people. STEM polling institute (1999, 2001) conducted a survey, which assessed perceptions of various threats to the Czech Republic. Most of the presented items expressed some kind of ethnic menace, whether coming from abroad or from domestic ethnic groups (additional items of this research are discussed in the following section devoted to worries about foreign countries and their influence). Ten-point scales were used (9 representing the strongest fear, 0 representing no fear at all). The threat of "the international organized crime" turned out to be the strongest with an average rating of 7.6 in 1999 and 7.9 in 2001, "increasing number of Chinese and Vietnamese entrepreneurs in our country" received rating of 6.6—same as "the inflow of refugees," "growing inflow of Moslems in Europe" was rated 6 in average, "the Roma minority in our country" 5.8, "the economic and political influence of Jews" was given the lowest ratings: 3.9 (CTK, 1999, May 18).

Immigrants were often considered a source of danger. This was expressed by nearly one-half of Czechs (49 percent) in a study by (IVVM, Jelínek, V., 2000). Only 6 percent respondents answered that immigrants might have a positive impact on Czech society. One-third claimed they perceived neither apparent danger nor benefit from immigrants and 12 percent chose not to answer. Only 14 percent supported the idea of foreigners coming to the Czech Republic to live and work. Thousands of hard working semi-legal immigrants (mainly Ukrainians, Chinese, and Vietnamese) were perceived with utmost distrust and suspicion of their (often imagined, but also often real) connections to organized crime. While 52 percent of respondents said that they were in favor of giving asylum to refugees who are under threat of death at their original homes, only 24 percent agreed that asylum should be granted to those fleeing political or other persecution, according to another survey by IVVM (CTK, 1997, November 21).

Worries about Foreign Countries

The Czech Republic is located in the middle of Europe and had a history of bitter experience with some of its neighbors (Klicperová, et al., 1997b). Just in the twentieth century, the Czech lands were invaded at least twice: During the Nazi occupation 1938–1945 and the Warsaw Pact invasion 1968–1989. Two large conflicts, World War I and the Balkan war of the 1990s, took place in the vicinity. Even though almost 40 percent of Czechs said in a poll conducted by GfK that they were afraid of an outbreak of a new world war (CTK, 1995, August 8), this is a common expression of a general people's concern, very common in other national polls. On the other hand, if people were asked prior to 2001 whether a threat of war was their prevailing concern, the answers were typically negative. For instance, in the 1990s, war was not among the most persistent worries of the country: In several surveys, no more than 3 percent of Czechs mentioned "war conflicts" as the most serious threat (Rezková, 2000a).

Yet, there were other, justified fears. When Radio Free Europe/Radio Liberty moved from Munich to the very center of Prague and decided to broadcast to Iran and Iraq, many Czechs expressed their concerns about possible terrorist attacks against the editorial offices—a Farsi service for

Iran and Radio Free Iraq in Arabic. According to a 1998 poll released by Sofres-Factum, 58 percent said they felt their fear of terrorism was justified. Nevertheless, 42 percent of people agreed with the broadcasts if they come from a secret location, while only 8 percent backed the idea of broadcasting from the central Prague locality (BBC, 1998, October 6).

A sizable proportion of the Czech population held beliefs about the dangers imposed by foreign intelligence. More than 38 percent of those polled by the Sofres-Factum agency said they thought foreign spies posed a threat to the Czech Republic. Over a third of respondents claimed that in their opinion, Russian agents (mostly spying Russian diplomats) were active in the Czech Republic.

The country's membership in NATO and inclusion to the European Union had less than unanimous support: Opinion polls conducted between 1998 and 1999 showed that one quarter to one third of Czechs did not support Czech membership in those international organizations (CTK, 1999, October 26; CTK, 1998).

As mentioned earlier, STEM agency (1999, 2001) asked the Czechs to assess several threats using a 10-point scale (0 meaning no fear at all). Various international issues and developments, such as "international organized crime" (which received the average 7.6), the "conflict in Kosovo" (7.0), "dominance of foreign capital" (6.1), and "economic subjugation of our country by Germany" (5.8) were among the most significant ones. The poll was reproduced in April 2001 - "international organized crime" appeared on top again (with average of 7.9 - 85 percent of respondents rating intense danger by high marks of 7, 8, and 9), new item "terrorism" was second (7.6 - 79 percent of respondents reporting intense threat), worries of concrete other countries included: "situation in Balkans" (6.6 - 57 percent), authoritarian or communist coup in the countries of the former USSR (6.1 - 49 percent), "the policy of the great world power of Russia" (6.1 - 48 percent), fear of "economic subjugation of our country by Germany" (5.6 or 40 percent), "the policy of the great world power of the U.S.A." (5.6 or 37 percent) and fear of "NATO influence on the politics of our country" (4.3 rating or only 19 percent respondents reporting intense threat).

What kind of attitudes did Czechs hold about foreign countries? In most opinion polls, large world powers or powerful neighbors such as Russia or Germany are among frequent "targets" of individual frustration. According to a 2000 poll, some Czechs felt menaced by the United States (18 percent), Germany (11), Ukraine (10) and China (4) (Hannon, 2000). In response to the question asked by STEM research center as to which country people believed represents the greatest military threat to the Czech Republic, 57 percent mentioned Russia, 20 percent said Germany, and 9 percent suggested the former Yugoslavia (CTK, 1994, February 22.)

Negative attitudes most often result from two factors: historical experience and the present politics.[5] The STEM agency made yearly inquiries into people's concerns about two neighbors: Russia and Germany. Attitudes of Czechs toward Germans showed clear change for the better in time. While in 1996 majority of Czechs (54 percent) perceived the Czech-German relations as "not good," in 1997 only 34 percent saw the relations in the same negative way. In the year 2000 as many as three quarters of Czechs perceived Czech-German relations as positive (STEM, 2000).

The data provided by STEM are generally in agreement with results obtained by other agencies (IVVM - Mišovič, 2000b). For example, 62 percent of respondents polled in March 2000 by IVVM saw Czech-German relations as "rather good" and an additional 15 percent as "very good," that is, 77 percent saw mutual relations in positive terms; only 14 percent negatively and 9 percent were not sure how to respond. Even a majority of communist supporters and over–60 age groups—many of whom resisted the German occupation during World War II or resented them for ideological reasons—have improved their perception of Germany.

A different attitudinal trend can be found in perception of Russia. The idea about existence of the "eastern" threat was typically voiced by the majority of Czech population. In surveys conducted between 1996 and 2000, people were asked the following question: "Some people are afraid of Russia. Do you personally think that Russia may represent a future threat to our republic?" A slight majority of respondents (51 to 58 percent over the 4-year period) believed it would. Only respondents older than 60 and people from the ideological left tended not to view Russia as a dangerous country. From the Czech communists only 30 percent perceived Russia as a threat (STEM, 2000).

In general, research showed that Germany was perceived more positively than Russia. In 1994, 57 percent named Russia as a source of threat, Germany was mentioned by 20 percent of respondents and Yugoslavia occurred in 9 percent of responses (CTK, 1994, February 22). In the IVVM surveys, about one third (34 percent in November 1994 and less, 29 percent, in July 1995) of Czechs feared a military threat from Russia. Only 13 percent expressed the same opinion toward Germany in 1994 and even less - 7 percent viewed Germany as a threat in 1995. Twenty-three percent said the Czech Republic faced no military threat at all (CTK, 1995, July 12). A poll by the Sociological Institute of the Academy of Sciences of the Czech Republic has revealed that almost two thirds of a thousand of respondents living along the German border said that Russia was a biggest danger for the Czech Republic while only 35 percent thought the same of Germany (CTK, 1998, April 12).

The structure and intensity of fears related to foreign countries has changed dramatically after the terrorist attack against the United States on September 11, 2001. An expeditious telephone survey by Median agency executed on the day following the assault illustrated the feelings of at least a limited quota sample of 352 respondents of the Czech Republic. People reported that when they found out about the attack, they felt most often: pity for lost human lives (61 percent), they experienced general feeling of fear (51), fear or terror that conflict may spread also to the Czech Republic (41), helplessness (35) and fury that somebody can do something so terrible (35). The majority worried that the event can in some way endanger also the Czech Republic (13 percent felt so "definitely," 43 percent in lesser intensity—"rather yes"). Still, a great number of respondents expressed some assurance that sufficient actions were undertaken in their country to avoid negative consequences of the attack (19 percent felt so definitely, 51 percent were less sure - responding "rather yes"). Most people felt "personally afraid" when they learned about the event (26 percent answered "definitely yes," 28 "rather yes," 25 "rather no" and 21 percent reported "definitely none" personal fear. Over two thirds of the respondents admitted that the terrorist attack against the United States "may cause some huge, global conflict, 3rd world war" - 16 percent "definitely" assumed so, 53 percent thought so with less assurance "rather yes," 26 meant "rather no" and only 5 percent were excluding a possibility of resulting world scale conflict by resolute "definitely no."

A similar survey about the Czech emotional reactions following the terrorist attacks against the United States was carried out 10 days after the attack by STEM (2001) agency, this time on a larger, representative sample and using face to face interviews. Eighty percent of respondents claimed that the attack against the United States was an event that concerns every citizen of the Czech Republic (only 60 percent of communists voiced the same opinion). Half of respondents also agreed with the participation of Czech troops in a fight against terrorism if necessary (approval was higher in better educated respondents and declined with age, women agreed less often and there was also a distinct relationship to party membership—communists agreeing the least, only in 28 percent). The majority (57 percent irrespective of demographic groups) predicted that there would be more terrorist attacks in the coming days and weeks and more than two thirds of respondents (69 percent) worried that the terrorist attacks may spill over into a world war conflict (women and the communists fearing the conflict more than other socio-demographic groups).

Resistance to anything "foreign" is not the case in the Czech Republic. People here, as well as in most European countries, can converse in two or three languages. Almost 50 percent of Czechs can converse in Russian or German, 30 percent can do it in English, and 7 percent in French or Spanish (CTK, 1999, May 10).

The majority of Czechs (65 percent) believed that a frequent use of English expressions in speech, signs, and the media was a natural phenomenon of the present, as poll conducted by the IVVM showed. However, 56 percent of the polled believed that "frequent usage of English expressions spoils the Czech language" (CTK, 1999, November 30). This concern does not necessarily lead to a specific conclusion: on one hand, the Czechs define their "Czechness" to a great degree by their language, yet people may dislike foreign neologisms in their native tongue for a variety of reasons besides xenophobia.

Environmental Concerns

Compared to many regions in Russia, Belarus, or Ukraine, the Czech Republic did not inherit devastating environmental problems. However, the environmental situation in the country was far from ideal. One of the biggest pollution-related problems of the past were brown coal burning power plants in Northern Bohemia. In previous years, they caused smog alerts not only in the adjacent neighborhoods, but also in areas far away, including Prague. Extensive air pollution by the local heavy industries, millions of automobiles that used leaded gasoline or gasoline and oil mix, as well as fall-out from neighboring plants in eastern Germany and Poland seriously affected the health of citizens and the flora of the country, especially its border forests. Soviet Army contingent with its military bases stretched through the entire territory of former Czechoslovakia was also a substantial source of pollution—water and soil contamination

In the 1970s and 1980s, even though the government largely suppressed information about environmental dangers, many concerned citizens were informed about the real state of the environment. In the 1980s—as in many other former socialist countries—various environmentalist movements and organizations brought together hundreds of concerned citizens, who started to pressure the regime by openly challenging its environmental policies.[6] The reform government together with citizen activists managed to improve the ecological situation in many regions. The industrial crisis facilitated restructuring of coal industry, closing of mines and metallurgic plants, the energy industry started to use cleaner technologies (for example, the air emissions of SO_2 in the Czech Republic dropped from 1,876 thousands of tons in 1990 to 443 thousands of tons in 1998 (Lynch, 2001). Citizens were financially motivated to use cleaner alternatives to coal burning,East German two stroke Trabant and Wartburg cars were gradually replaced by new domestic Škodas and Western imports, which used unleaded gasoline. The industrial areas of the Northern Bohemia, Northern Moravia and Prague underwent a major cleanup. Successful recycling programs were launched.

Overall, during the first eleven years of the transitional period, Czechs expressed strong concerns about environmental problems. (See table 3.3). There was a dissatisfaction with the overall state of the environment: In one poll, over 55 percent of Czechs were dissatisfied with the state of the environment in the country (CTK poll, 1996, June 18). However, more positive opinions were expressed when people were asked about the environment in their own neighborhood (i.e., the quality of the environment which they new best). When judging their own neighborhood, majority of the Czechs was also dissatisfied in the early post-revolutionary years, yet since 1993 on there were more people satisfied than dissatisfied (in 2000, satisfaction was reported by 55 percent and dissatisfaction by only 13 percent of respondents). Although it is difficult to make direct assessments, positive environmental changes were probably a factor in the 4-year increase in life expectancy among Czechs in the 1990s—a striking positive result, especially with respect to the fact that life expectancy declined in many other countries undergoing process of transformation in the same period.

Computer age brought new challenges. As in other countries, some Czechs feared computers. When polled in late 1997, 10 percent of respondents admitted fear of computers and additional 21 percent acknowledged their dislike of them, 44 percent claimed they did not mind the work with computers, while 21 percent answered they enjoyed working with them, four percent chose the answer (only one was allowed) that they could not imagine their lives without computers any more according to a survey by AISA agency (CTK, 1998, February 25). A certain part of the population expressed their concern about potential dangers of the Internet. One of the concerns was individual privacy: According to a 1999 poll by the Dema agency, 35 percent of Internet users worried about their personal privacy (CTK, 1999, June 8).

Fears in the Context of Public Opinion

A rapid swing from hopelessness to an extended euphoria, then relatively rapid decline to disenchantment and then slow rebuilding of trust and optimism: that seems to be a prevailing course of emotions the Czech society went through. Opinion polls illustrate this course. For as many as six years since the Velvet Revolution, the Czechs were in love with their politicians (IVVM 1996)—majorities openly expressing their stable trust to the government and five or six leading politicians. How-

Table 3.3 Environmental Concerns of Czechs (1989–2000)

Type of environmental fears or concerns	*Year*	*Percent*
Fears of potential environmental problems[a]	1989	76
Worries of consequences of the nuclear disaster in Chernobyl[b]	1991	20
Current environmental problems perceived as "very urgent"[c]	1995	54
Fear of an environmental catastrophe[d]	1995	23
Worries about the price hike due to the flood of 1997[e]	1997	43
Worries about economic troubles due to the flood of 1997[c]	1997	49
Fears of potential environmental problems[a]	1999	28
Worry that the 1999 sun eclipse would have a negative impact on human life[f]	1999	20
Worry that the 1999 sun eclipse could be followed by big natural disasters[f]	1999	10
Worry that the 1999 sun eclipse could result in the end of the world[f]	1999	6
Current environmental problems perceived as "very urgent"[c]	2000	45

[a]Poll by: IVVM. Source: CTK, 1999, November 11 (Sample: Czechoslovakia)
[b]Poll by: Institute for the Research in Public. Source: Opinion. CTK, 1991, May 31 (Sample: Czechoslovakia)
[c]Poll by: IVVM. Source: IVVM—Rezková (2000a)
[d]Poll by: GFK. Source: CTK, 1995, August 8
[e]Poll by: Factum, Source: CTK, 1997, September 13
[f]Poll by: Sofres-Factum. Source: CTK, 1999, August 7

ever, at the tenth anniversary of regaining freedom, despite the achieved progress, as many as 78 percent expressed the distrust of the government, 80 percent distrust of the Chamber of Deputies and an equal percentage also distrust of the Senate (IVVM, 2001). A poll taken at the same time, in November of 1999, revealed that 73 percent of respondents stated that the moral climate in the country had not improved since November 1989. Only 29 percent of those polled believed that courts were impartial, forty-nine percent of Czechs expressed no trust in the police and the army. Typically, pensioners, unemployed, and blue-collar workers were most critical of government institutions (CTK, 1998, May 19). Conversely, market-orientated people tended to be more optimistic about the overall situation in the country but a negative assessment of the moral climate prevailed even among them (CTK, 1999, November 17).

In the mid-1990s, a five percent growth of Czech economy was set to outpace western European averages. Unemployment was in low single digits. Inflation was down from double-digit figures in previous years to a bearable 8.5 percent level. It was high by Western standards, but lower than the rate in Poland, Hungary, or Russia (McCathie, 1996). Despite these achievements, as mentioned earlier in this chapter and will be referred to elsewhere in the book, the "reform fatigue" develops among the population of any country that is undergoing fundamental transformations. Many failed to adjust to the requirements of a new capitalist society, and many people had higher expectations than the reality turned out to be. As a result, disappointment, disenchantment, and pessimism set in. Interestingly though, the Czechs seemed to be more often satisfied than dissatisfied when they were asked for their personal perspective and their concrete personal experience than if they are asked about their evaluation of the society in general. This proved to be the case whether they are asked about how good was the previous year (Rezková, 2000b), how they perceive the quality of interpersonal relations (Kučerová, 1999), or (as mentioned earlier) how satisfied they are with the quality of the environment.

The level of disenchantment was lower in the Czech Republic than in other transitional societies that witnessed communist comebacks. Careful monetary policy, and consideration of people's expectations had a positive impact on people's coping with transition. The euphoric nation easily withstood the initial shock of price deregulation and early phases of privatization, then, during the disenchanted years, the reforms were cushioned, and many important areas of expenses, such as rent and energy, were still subsidized by the state. After all, in the beginning of the transition more than three quarters of Czechs believed that the state should exercise control over rent and municipal maintenance fees (CTK, 1993, August 27). It is an issue of discussions among the politicians and economists whether this gentle strategy instead of continuation of the shock therapy was the best choice.

President Václav Havel, former dissident writer and leader of the 1989 Velvet Revolution, did not escape the destiny of many other charismatic leaders of the transitional period. Once he was generally admired, respected, and idolized as a politician and as a man. In the late 1990s he was frequently misunderstood and criticized. His popularity ratings fell from post-revolutionary 90 percent (AISA, Penn & Schoen, 1990) to 46 percent at the end of the 1990s (Holley, 1999). Yet, as people were coming to terms with transition and at the break of millennium started to recover from their disenchantment, they also rediscovered their president's exceptionality - as reflected in the polls. IVVM reports from September 2001 indicate that since September 1999, trust in president Havel had not dropped below 50 percent (IVVM -Červenka 2001).

So, the Czech emotional pendulum was for a long time (1989–1996) high on the positive side during the post-revolutionary euphoria. Then, as a reaction to the economic crisis and financial scandals of the leading political party, national emotions swung in the opposite direction toward the so called "bad mood" ("*blbá Nálada*") since 1997 for the rest of the decade. The end of year 1999 seemed to have brought recovery to responsible activism, positive thinking, and realistic optimism and that reflected also in a slow but pronounced return of trust to the political institutions: the Government, the Chamber of Deputies, the Senate as well as the President (IVVM, Červenka 2001). Yet, slow and hesitant return of optimism was being halted mainly by realistic worries about international politics—actions at Balkans and, most importantly, the outbreak of war on terrorism.

Such emotional fluctuation should not have been a surprise. Many scholars in the past have described analogous emotional sways in transforming societies: Alexis de Tocqueville (1997) was among the first who described the dramatic rise of expectations in a previously apathetic population. J. Davies (1997) described the activating potential of the gap between what people want and what they get. Feierabend and colleagues (1972) suggested that fast unexpected change to the better will be followed by unrealistic growth of expectations and inevitable frustration.

Conclusion: Some Perspectives on Czech Fears

Thinking about the fears of the Czechs—as well as other national groups presented in this book—in terms of statistical national averages or standard "modal" citizens requires a great deal of abstraction. Different social groups within national samples express different attitudes. For example, the most active and successful types of the Czech society—the young entrepreneurs—report no significant fears. On the other hand, those who are socially passive, less educated, or belong to lower socio-economic strata tend to report more fears. There is an age gap in responses: Young people typically tend to be fearless (majority of teenage respondents and more than 40 percent of people in their 20s reported no fears). A small gender gap was also revealed: In their answers, men tended to be less worrying than women. More fears were revealed among those Czech citizens who considered themselves left-wing, compared to other political groups (CTK, 1993, December 9).

Although the small Czech nation had a long history of difficult struggle for survival, the nation's experience provided the Czechs with a sense of collective identity and achievement. Czechs are aware of the great heritage of the Czech kingdom—Prague was once a center of the Holy Roman Empire. At the same time, Czechs feel secure about their democratic roots. As mentioned before, most consider the first Czechoslovak republic (1918–1938) one of the finest periods in their history (Mišovič,

2000b)[7] and a sound base for future building of a democratic nation. Sense of ethnic identity and benevolence might have contributed to the Czech willingness to respect the Slovak push for their sovereignty and the "velvet divorce" (Klicperova et al., 1997b).

Overall, most worries and fears of Czechs living in a post-communist society were based on rational evaluations of the progress of domestic transition as well as the international situation but balanced by strong belief in the continuation of the democratic process.

Notes

1. Although all Czechs were subject to approximately 40 years of communist molding, the post-communist syndrome was not a widespread occurrence. After all, communist ideals did not conquer the vast majority of Czechs; the nation was forced to import communism at the stage of exhaustion in the aftermath of Nazism and accompanied by bitter memory of being betrayed by democratic allies.
2. For example, the price of the *Škoda Favorit,* a popular automobile, jumped from 65,000 crowns to about 115,000 crowns in 1990, whereas the average monthly wage hovered at about 3,500 crowns.
3. Between 1997 and 2000, only 2 to 3 percent mentioned "crime" when answering the question: "When you give a thought to your current situation, what worries you the most? Are you afraid of something? If yes, what is it?"
4. Several factors contributed to the development of crime-related worries in the Czech population. Shortly after the revolution, the government granted an amnesty to most criminals detained in Czechoslovakian prisons. After their release, most of these individuals received little guidance and assistance. Many of them could not adjust to the new social and returned to crime as the only known (to them) source of income. The ongoing privatization and economic reform undoubtedly contributed to "white-collar crimes," such as corruption and fraud. Politicians, in general, failed to pay serious attention to these crimes. For instance, former Prime Minister Pithart, despite far-reaching plans, stopped short of fulfilling them. Another Prime Minister, social democrat Zeman, used a plea to fight against corruption mostly for the achievement of his electoral goals.
5. Of course, there are more than two factors that affect people's opinions about other countries. Among them there are political, socio-economic, psychological, and ideological influences. (See, for example, Shiraev & Zubok, 2001.)
6. Concerns about an unlivable environment inspired the foundation of an ecological Green party; however, because practically all political parties included environmental concerns to their platforms, the Green party lost its popular appeal and never gained substantial power again.

7. The fact that even the young generation holds the memory of the First Czechoslovak Republic in high esteem was documented also by our pilot study of the subject. We asked over 100 Czech students of the Faculty of Social Sciences of Charles University to draw a "Lifeline of the Czech nation" (the ups and downs of the Czechs during the twentieth century and near future. The high is in prime of the First Republic, the second high was placed to the future, another ascend is in the late 1960s (prior to the Soviet invasion of 1968) while periods of communism and Nazi occupation make the lows. These results correspond with our earlier pilot studies in which university students were placing the absolute high to the era of the First Republic and high school students saw it in the most recent period following the Velvet Revolution or in he First Republic. In all student groups there was always an optimistic outlook to the future (Klicperová et al. 1999). Even though the young and the educated have the most optimistic views, these results should not be generalized to the whole society.

Chapter 4

Poland: Fears in Transition

Urszula Jakubowska

Located at the borderland between Western and Eastern civilizations, Poland, as well as some other post-communist countries, such as Lithuania, Latvia, Estonia, Slovakia, and the Czech Republic, had a relatively short history as a sovereign nation-state (Jalowiecki, 1996). After the period of great military expansion and economic growth of the sixteenth and seventeenth centuries, Poland entered a long period of foreign domination and suppression. For almost 140 years—from 1779, with the exception of short periods of independence—this country was partitioned among three European empires: Russia, Prussia, and Austria. During all these years, any attempt to fight for independence and against oppression were overpowered by the neighboring countries, which pursued policies aimed at eradicating Polish ethnic identity, culture, and language. Poland finally gained its independence after the collapse of the Russian and German empires and the ending of World War I by the Treaty of Versailles of 1919. The independence lasted for 20 years until Poland was occupied by Nazi Germany in 1939. After the end of World War II, Poland, for 45 years, fell into military, economic, and political dependence on the Soviet Union. The Polish United Working Party ruled the country until 1989, when the communist authorities and the growing opposition started negotiating about running the country together. These negotiations resulted in the first democratic elections organized in the country since World War II. They resulted in a victory by the opposition consolidated around the *Solidarity* trade union and Lech Walesa, the charismatic leader who was regarded in the West as a symbol of Polish democratic rebirth. The transitional period of the 1990s was characterized by the establishment of democratic principles of government, promotion of basic human liberties, and further distancing from Russia, the culmination of which was the acceptance of Poland into NATO. As several other post-communist countries, Poland also experienced a left-wing comeback into legislative and executive branches of government in Warsaw and in many Polish regions. This was a result of many voters' disappointment with the way government handled domestic problems and people's unwillingness to give up major social security benefits.

Hopes, Fears, and Disappointments

Overall, people in Poland expressed many of their fears and concerns in the ways in which many people in different countries express their worries. Typically, for instance, in the majority of surveys on this topic, most respondents mention personal misfortunes—such as injury and illness—as prime sources of their concerns (Strzeszewski, 1999a; Wciorka, 2000). There is not anything specifically "Polish" in these opinions and attitudes: People everywhere in the world tend to express concerns about quality of their health. There was, however, one health-related area that may reflect one of the serious and long-term problems Poland faced through the years: substance abuse and addiction. According to CBOS polls, for example, among top three most important problems of Poland in 1992, 18 percent of people mentioned substance addiction, including mainly alcoholism (*Rzeczpospolita,* n. 212, September 9, 1992). Four years later, according to a 1996 survey, people's expressed worries about alcohol and drug problems practically did not change (*Gazeta Wyborcza,* 1996, n. 55, March 5).

In the early 1990s, environmental problems were also mentioned among the most urgent issues with which society has to deal. For example, in 1992, 31 percent of Poles chose environment as one among three of the most urgent problems of their country (*Rzeczpospolita,* 1992, n. 212, September 9). In 1993, 20 percent of Poles considered environment the most urgent national problem (PAP, 1993, August 13.) One third of the respondents believed that environmental pollution should be one of Poland's most essential concerns in 1993. However, contrary to what people in neighboring Ukraine and Belarus felt, fears of nuclear accidents were practically insignificant according to survey conducted in 1994 (*Rzeczpospolita,* 1994, n. 38, February 15).

As in almost every post-communist society of the 1990s, people in Poland had to cope with an unprecedented surge of criminal activities. In a CBOS poll taken in 1995 and 1998, more than three quarters of people said that their country was not a safe place to live in. As many as 28 percent of the surveyed in 1994 feared organized crime (*Rzeczpospolita,* 1994,

n. 38, February 15). Critical opinion about police and their ineffectiveness in curbing crime was expressed by 60 percent of respondents in 1998 as opposed to 34 percent who expressed the opposite opinion (*Prawo i Gospodarka,* 1998, n. 75, April 7). At the same time—and this trend in opinions is found in other countries' surveys—72 percent of respondents said that they felt safe in their own home. This opinion about personal safety in one's own home was supported by 84 percent of rural residents, 76 percent of small town inhabitants, and 56 percent of city dwellers.

To understand the nature of fears and worries about different aspects of society it is important to take a look at people's assessments of the transitional process in general, their expectations and hopes. Polish people have a history of civil resistance to oppressive governments and skepticism toward authorities (Toranska, 1989, 1994.) Since the late 1980s, critical appraisals of government, public officials, and specific policies could be voiced freely. Unlike in the Czech Republic, the "honeymoon" period was relatively short: According to a 1991 poll, 51 percent of respondents suggested that the situation in Poland was headed in the wrong direction and deteriorated rapidly. One third of Poles feared that things might get worse (*Gazeta Wyborcza,* 1991, n. 140, June 18). The belief in rising social disapproval accompanied by fear that the current "sacrifices will not produce any improvement" was expressed by 56 percent of the respondents (*Gazeta Wyborcza,* 1991, n.73, March 27).

As surveys from 1993 to 1995 demonstrate, the term "democracy" was associated mainly with a welfare state and to a lesser degree with free market and the developing democratic institutions such as free elections, independent courts, and civil liberties (Reykowski, 1995). These diverse interpretations of democracy were displayed both by ordinary people as well as political elites (Jakubowska, 1999a, 1999b). Individual differences in interpreting democracy were related to specific expectations people had of the democratic state. When Poles were asked how they understand the obligation of the state to its citizens, the majority of the respondents repeatedly emphasized that the state should respect above all social and economic rights (including the right to prosperity) more than political and religious freedoms. In other words, most Poles expected the state to continue to play an active role in the organization of social life (Roguska 2000b).

However, the actual process of transformation in Poland went in the opposite direction. Major social policies were limiting the influence of the state on the country's economy and social life. In fact, this has been the purpose of the 1990s' reforms: privatization and re-privatization of state-owned means of production, the reorganization of the social-security system, education, and health service. This discrepancy between many people's expectations of what a democratic state should be and the evaluation of the actual effects of the transformation can be illustrated by the results of the following 2000 poll (Sek, 2000). When people were asked a question: "Are you satisfied with the way democracy functions in Poland?," only 27 percent of the respondents gave affirmative answers. Indicating their disappointment with the political transformation in society, 84 percent of people in this survey said that they "have no possibility to influence the solutions of societal problems."

However, at the same time, Poles generally support democracy as a political system. When asked: "Was it worthwhile to change the political system in Poland 10 years ago?" two-thirds of the 1999 national sample agreed. Among the supporters of democracy, the largest was the group with college education (91 percent), high-school education (79 percent), vocational education (66 percent), and middle-school education (48 percent). The weakest support came from farmers and unskilled workers, 41 percent and 38 percent respectively. Thirty percent of positive answers came from respondents who identified themselves with the left-wing ideology (Pankowski, 1999a). Support for the new political system was expressed mainly by those people who benefited the most from the societal transformation. They were hardly affected by unemployment, quickly adjusted to market changes, and began to earn relatively high incomes (Czapinski, 1996). Self-declared satisfaction with life in this group was also highest among other socioeconomic groups (Pankowski, 2000; Roguska, 1999).

Unfortunately, those who did not receive immediate economic benefits were mostly farmers and unskilled workers. The processes of privatization of all Polish industries, closures of unprofitable factories and coal mines, resulted in massive layoffs and caused many workers to migrate and look for new jobs in new places (Czapinski, 1996). For Polish farmers, the lack of resources, entrepreneurial skills, and low level of education were the major obstacles that slowed down their adaptation to a free-market economy. The limitation of state subsidies to the country's agricultural sector significantly increased the costs of production. Unprotected by tariffs, they faced the consequences of unrestricted international trade that brought to Poland high-quality agricultural products from abroad. This resulted in bankruptcies of many farms (Gucwa-Lesny, 1996).

Similar to many transitional post-communist democracies, the Polish transformation meant a significant departure from an egalitarian system of distribution of resources. New policies substantially reduced government's involvement in the process of providing social security benefits to its citizens. As a result, social and political reforms were subjects of different—and often opposite—assessments from different groups of population.

People's expectations and fears, to a substantial degree, were based on how individuals viewed their own situation and societal transition in general.

To simplify the analysis of people's worries, let us pay attention to at least three categories. The first will be concerns about the economy and the individual's socioeconomic situation. The second category includes concerns about internal political situation. The third category is related to international developments around Poland.

Worries about Economic Issues

The process of political and social transformation in Poland started in the time of an acute economic crisis followed by a long recession lasting until 1992. Only in the mid-1990s, ordinary citizens could feel early effects of economic reforms. Economic growth started to pick up: real gross domestic product in 1994 rose by 5 percent, by 7 percent in 1995, and in 1996 it grew 6 percent. From 1990 until 1996 10 percent of households bought cars, 26 percent bought video equipment, 10 percent purchased CD players and computers, 30 percent got televisions, 15 percent purchased cable TV (Kolarska-Bobinska, 1997). From the beginning of the 1990s, unemployment was relatively under control. As a result, in 1999, only 28 percent of Poles evaluated their own financial situation as "rather bad" or "bad." About half—51 percent of Poles—judged their financial situation as "neither good nor bad," and 21 percent as "rather good," or "good." These numbers reflected significantly better self-evaluations than in neighboring Russia, Ukraine, and Belarus.

The feeling of financial security of Polish families, however, was not reflective of overall worry-free life. In 1992, two thirds of people chose unemployment among the top three most important problems that the country faced and 59 percent also included low wages in this category (*Rzeczpospolita,* 1992, September 9).

Moreover, surveys conducted in the 1990s suggest that economic concerns and living conditions were on top of the list in many Polish homes. A survey carried out by the OBOP polling center showed that 68 percent of Poles believed things in Poland were going in the wrong direction. Seven out of ten respondents believed Poland was in a state of economic crisis. More than one half of the respondents (52 percent) feared their living conditions would worsen in the forthcoming three years (PAP, 2000, July 12). In 1999, only 12 percent of Poles declared they were not afraid of poverty, 33 percent agreed with the statement "I am not afraid of poverty, although I am worried that our financial situation can become worse," 37 percent chose the statement "I am afraid of poverty, but I think we will manage somehow," 17 percent expressed their fear and helplessness saying "I am afraid of poverty and I don't know how to manage it" (Wciorka, 1999a). Financial self-evaluation of the Poles remained low. Only one person in seven (14 percent) considered himself or herself and the family to be an economic "winner" of the transformation, while twice as many Poles (29 percent) claimed that they lost as a result of the transformation (Wciorka, 1999b). In 1999 and 2000, about one third of Poles referred to their financial situation as a source of worry (Strzeszewski, 1999a; Wciorka, 2000).

A 1994 poll conducted by CBOS revealed that among the most worrisome problems were: unemployment, low wages, overly high prices, and incompetent people in the government. Unemployment was seen as the most troublesome problem by 65 percent of the participants of the poll. Low wages and high prices were mentioned by 54 percent. Those who worried most about their financial situation were, first of all, respondents between 24 and 35 years of age who had low-level education or unskilled workers (*Rzeczpospolita,* 1994, n. 38, February 15). Another CBOS poll revealed that 40 percent of Poles worried about personal poverty and 39 percent feared that they might not be able to afford the costs of medical treatment and 37 percent were afraid of losing their job. A fall in living standards was reported as a source of fear for 31 percent (*Gazeta Wyborcza,* 1996, n. 55, March 5).

According to a 1997 CBOS survey, 37 percent of people in Poland believed that the privatization of a state enterprise was disadvantageous for its employees, while 11 percent of respondents feared privatization would actually lead to the collapse of their enterprises (*Rzeczpospolita,* 1997, n. 110, May 13). In a poll taken in December 1997, after the government announced plans to raise price on several goods at the beginning of 1998, about 88 percent of respondents especially feared the announced hikes in electric energy prices (*Prawo i Gospodarka,* 1998, n. 8, January 9)[1].

The sense of personal loss or defeat may be related to the perception of a considerable diversity of income in the 1990s. As a result of the ongoing societal transformation, quick enrichment of a few social groups was accompanied by a dramatic loss of income among many other groups. Successful private entrepreneurs were perhaps in the best position, while farmers, pensioners, and the unemployed were in the worst (Gucwa-Lesny, 1996). For example, in 1990 the ratio of the highest to the lowest incomes per family was 1:8; in 1996 it was 1:11 (Kolarska-Bobinska, 1997). It is interesting that the perceived difference in income, according to people's assessments, was much higher—1: 21.5 (Wciorka, 1999b).

When asked about inequality, the Poles generally accept differences in income among people. In 2000, 81 percent of people agreed with the statement: "Those who work well should be paid well if we want to have prosperity in Poland." Only 14 percent of respondents strongly disagreed with this statement (Falkowska, 2000). However, 92 percent of Poles believe that "the differences between the rich and the poor are too large," and 76 percent of Poles agreed with the following statement: "It is a duty of the government to reduce the differences between the people who earn a lot and the people who earn little" (Falkowska, 1998).

Perhaps the renewed attractiveness of the left-wing political forces reemerged in the early 1990s, reflecting people's fears that, despite rising industrial production and high rates of economic growth, unemployment would continue to rise beyond an already high 15 percent level. The leftward tilt also was based on fears that the future should bring the dismantling of the social welfare programs and would eliminate practically unlimited access to free schooling and health-care facilities (Bobinski and Robinson, 1993). Almost 47 percent of the population in Poland in the late 1990s expressed their worries about losing their job and 73 percent supposed they would have problems finding a similar job if they were laid off (Dereczynski, 1998). Fear of unemployment was expressed in almost one third of Polish respondents in a 1999 comparative poll conducted by IVVM, which revealed that fears of unemployment were higher in Poland than in neighboring Hungary and the Czech Republic (CTK, June 16, 1999). In 1999, 42 percent of the polled feared for their family members' health, and 31 percent voiced concern over their material situation. Fear of losing a job was expressed by 21 percent (PAP, 1999, March 17).

In a 1992 survey, 46 percent of respondents, who were selecting one answer from a variety of options, chose the statement that democracy is useful when it "brings prosperity," as opposed to 18 percent of respondents who considered democracy is useful when it provides a "realization of freedom" (Kolarska-Bobinska, 1997). It is understandable that for those who did not find prosperity for themselves—or at least did not achieve financial security during the transitional period—fears and concerns about the whole course of events should be inevitable.

Fears about Government and Society

During more than 10 years of the transformation process, the Polish cabinet changed seven times and local governments were replacing one another nearly as frequently as the cabinet ministers in Warsaw. Facing such instability, Poles' fears of political destabilization at home seemed objectively justified. Around one quarter of Poles (29 percent in 1999 and 22 percent in 2000) expressed their worries about a possibility of social unrest (Strzeszewski, 1999a, Wciorka, 2000). Fears of public unrest were mentioned by only 14 percent of people in 1992 (*Rzeczpospolita,* 1992, n.

212, September 9). However, protests did not go beyond rallies and strikes. Overall, in 2000, 58 percent of Poles were disaffected with their government in Warsaw (DPA, 2000, August 10). Moreover, most people formed a stable negative attitude toward politicians of all levels (Falkowska, 1999).

Despite these developments, Poland continued to be a stable and developing democracy. The worries of most people typically referred to the course of public debates about what democratic path Poland should accept and how to further pursue the transformation process. Generally, the conflict about a political shape of the state was concentrated around the question of whether the state should be pluralistic, secular, and open to the world or whether Poland should be a Catholic state with a strong adherence to the nationalist idea. Various groups of people for various reasons feared the government's final embrace of one way or the other (Boski, 1991; Markowski, 1997; Jakubowska, 1999a, b).

Economic situation was another source of debates and disagreement in opinions. Although there was a common view that the old centrally planned economy turned out to be inefficient and had to be replaced with a free-market economy, still, the dispute continued over the pace of privatization and the acceptable level of state interventionism (Morawski, 1996). As in other transitional democracies, there were supporters in Poland of slow, cautious, and "evolutionary" economic changes. On the other hand, there were supporters of more radical changes. Unfortunately, it should be stressed that, unlike in most developed democracies, political conflicts among individuals and groups in many transitional democracies tend not to end in a compromise: The opponent is often treated as the enemy who has to be defeated by all means.

Incompetence of the government was named by 43 percent of Poles among the three most urgent problems that the country faced in 1992 (*Rzeczpospolita,* 1992, n. 212, September 9). Incompetent people in the government were a major source of worries for 30 percent of participants, according to a poll by CBOS in 1993 (*Rzeczpospolita,* 1994, n. 38, February 15). Three years later, this type of concern was expressed by 32 percent of Poles, according to CBOS polling service (*Gazeta Wyborcza,* 1996, n. 55, March 5).

Fears of a particular party taking over the government played some role in people's voting behavior. For example, in a 1997 poll, when participants were asked which party's election victory they fear the most, the opinions split: 24 percent of respondents mentioned the Democratic Left Alliance, and 20 percent named the Solidarity Elections Action (*Gazeta Wyborcza,* 1997, n. 200, August 28). The victory of Aleksandr Kwasniewski, head of a left-wing party (which, in fact, was the reformed Communist Party), in the 1995 presidential election reawakened fears among his opponents of the communists' comeback to power. Fear of a communist "restoration" was fueled by the prospects of a coalition between the former communists, populists, and nationalists. However, these worries did not have a profound effect on most citizens of Poland. Even though Lech Walesa based his 1995 presidential campaign on evoking in people various fears of communists getting back to high offices, the majority of voters still voted for Kwasniewski, who ran his campaign on attractive ideas of social democracy and social protection for ordinary people. In addition, some positive aspects of the new situation were perceived: first, communism in many people's view, was associated still with the liberation from the Nazi occupation; second, the slogans of social equality and free education for all created opportunities for promotion for enormous groups of people (Rakowski, 1998).

International Contacts and Fears of Losing Independence

According to a poll conducted by CBOS between 13 and 16 September, 2001, Over 51 per cent of Poles (from a national sample of 1,225) believed that Poland could be a target of terrorist attacks, while 37 per cent think that this country is not threatened by terrorists. Sixty-five per cent of Poles are of the opinion that the recent developments in the United States might lead to a world conflict.

In Poland, opinions about international relations are polarized between integrative tendencies and isolationist attitudes. The first tendency dominates in official Polish politics. Supporters of the idea that Poland should be a country open to the world believe that closer international ties are a good chance for fast economic and scientific development. International cooperation is also good for maintaining national security. Poles' integrative attitudes are manifested, for example, in general approval of Poland's membership in NATO and the European Union (Strzezewski, 1999b, 2000). By contrast, in isolationists' view, membership in NATO is not a guarantee of the country's security. Moreover, it increases the threat of losing sovereignty and independence.

The perceived threat is justified with the following argumentation. First, Russia's furious protests against NATO expansion indicated that the Kremlin has not yet renounced its aspirations in Eastern Europe (Strzeszewski, 1999b). Thus, Poland's membership in NATO created additional tensions with the eastern neighbor. Second, the United States is frequently involved in military conflicts, and Poland's membership in NATO entails participation of Polish troops in these operations. Apart from understandable reluctance to commit men and women to fight in foreign lands, the very idea of military actions in other countries activates an embarrassing historic memory: At least twice in history, Polish troops participated in the suppression of democratic opposition in Hungary and Czechoslovakia in 1956 and 1968 as part of the military operation of the Warsaw Pact commanded by the Soviet Union. In many people's view, Poland may become a puppet in the hands of an omnipotent master from overseas. Fears of a diminishing independence are reflected in a letter sent to the editors of a left-wing magazine: "This time we are to fight under the command of a new allied power—the United States—naturally in the name of their imperialist goals of a superpower. Whenever servility of Polish elites became the reasons of the State, the nation paid for their political stupidity with a loss, or at best with a nagging restriction of sovereignty. So I am calling: Social democrats, come to your senses!" (*Dzis,* n. 6, 1999).

There is little surprise in attributing imperialist aspirations to the United States. In 1999, Kofta and Sedek conducted a study on a national sample of Poles who were given a list of the following ethnic and religious groups: Americans, Chinese, French, Japanese, Germans, Poles, Russians, and Jews. The respondents were asked two questions. The first question inquired whether a particular group aims to rule the world. The second question asked whether these groups desire to play the decisive role in the international financial institutions. It was found that the largest number of respondents (56 percent) indicated Americans—as the nation—who aim at ruling the world (table 4.1).

The results of this study may suggest that the Poles, answering survey questions, were mostly concerned about the imperialist aspirations of Americans and Germans and the financial aspirations of Americans, Germans, Jews, and Japanese.

However, these concerns may have little influence on attitudes about specific issues. For example, most Poles indicate the three largest neighbors—Germany, Russia and Ukraine—as the most appreciated economic partners in spite of all negative historical experience accumulated during the years of post-Soviet transition. In 2000, 69 percent of Poles believed that a friendly relationship with Russia is possible. However, it should be emphasized that in the same study, two thirds of respondents feared a possibility of a rebirth of Russia's dominance over Poland. Readiness for cooperation was increasing in attitudes toward Germany and Ukraine. For example, in 1997, 58 percent of Poles believed that reconciliation with Ukrainians was possible and in 2000, such an opinion was expressed by 67 percent of respondents. In 1990, only 47 percent of Poles believed that reconciliation with Germany was possible, while in 2000 this opinion was shared by 76 percent of respondents (Strzeszewski, 2000). Nevertheless, there was a sense of an incoming threat from Germany, especially after cer-

Table 4.1 Percent of Poles Who Agree that the Following Groups Attempt to Dominate the World and Play the Decisive Role in the International Financial Institutions. Source: Kofta and Sedek (1999).

	Dominate the World	*Financial Institutions*
Americans	56	77
Germans	53	68
Russians	36	30
Jews	43	57
Japanese	33	60
Chinese	26	19
French	6	26
Poles	3	19

tain groups across the border began demanding compensation for thousands of ethnic Germans who were forced to emigrate from Poland after World War II. Amid optimistic feelings about the relationship with Germany, many Polls were also aware of a surge of ultra-right rhetoric in its western neighbor. Statements that Germany was not responsible for World War II and that its eastern border with Poland should be redrawn began to appear in German nationalist newspapers (Sherwell, 1998). Right-wing parties, such as the German People's Union, began to gain votes in local elections in German lands bordering Poland. However, there was no real threat from Germany, and people's worries turned out to be short-lived. A 1996 Demoskop poll showed Poles were more afraid of Russia than of Germany. As many as 57 percent of those polled in 1996 mentioned political threats coming from Russia. Russian military threats were mentioned by 61 percent, and an economic threat was mentioned by 40 percent. Germany was seen as a political threat by 16 percent; 18 percent referred to Germany as a military threat. Thirty-eight percent of respondents said Germany was an economic threat to Poland. As many as 47 percent of those surveyed believed threats from Russia had been growing in the 1990s, while only 5 percent perceived the same trend regarding Germany (*Zycie Warszawy,* 1996, March 6). According to a survey conducted by CBOS in 1995, 72 percent of Poles believed that in the near future Russia would be inclined to regain the former Soviet Union's influence in Eastern and Central Europe, compared to 39 percent in 1993 (PAP, 1995, July 31).

There was a steady increase of anxiety concerning the European Union in the 1990s. As early as 1994, 77 percent of Poles supported Poland's membership in the European Union. Six years later, in 2000, the support diminished to 59 percent (Roguska, 2000c). A critical attitude toward cooperation with the EU was observed mainly among farmers, who suffered considerable economic losses due to a free flow of foreign agricultural products to the Polish market. A survey conducted by the Institute for Public Affairs in 1999 showed that most Polish farmers feared free-market competition, inevitable if Poland joined the European Union. The survey also showed that 90 percent of Polish farmers knew nothing or very little about the European Union and the potential advantages of EU integration (*Polish News Bulletin,* 1999). On the other hand, well-educated and well-to-do respondents showed the strongest support of Poland's integration with the European Union.

Opponents of the integration with the European Union also argue that stronger member states will dominate and take advantage of weaker states, including Poland. Right-wing politicians, adducing Polish history, warn that the diktat that was previously associated with Moscow now will be replaced with the diktat from Brussels. In addition, opponents argue, open borders and freedom of travel will dissolve already weakened national identity. Conservatives of all political parties are also concerned about the patterns of the "Western" lifestyle actively promoted in Poland, such as celebrations of holidays that have not been part of the Polish tradition, including St. Valentine's Day and Halloween. Many church leaders and conservative individuals worried that the opening of Polish society to Western influences and values would prove a greater challenge than 45 years of ideological pressure of Soviet and communist ideology (Engelberg, 1991). Indeed, Polish people willingly accept not only Western customs but also the language. For example, internet sites, shop signs, and labels written in foreign languages (usually in English) were so common that a special legislation about the protection of the Polish language was passed, which established the Polish-only rule.

Those who feared Poland's membership in NATO argued that this military and political bloc would not be eager to defend Poland in case of an emergency. They agued that in 1939, despite given promises and signed agreements, when the country was under Hitler's attack nobody came to rescue Poland. Opponents of Polish marriage with the European Union also warned that the membership would not make Poland rich overnight (Stylinski, 1999). Polish accession to the European Union was feared by many of those who believed that the relatively low cost of Polish land and dwellings would quickly attract foreign buyers, especially from Germany, who may soon control large territories in Poland, thus threatening Polish economic independence. A great deal of resentment toward foreigners buying land in Poland was demonstrated in a 1996 CBOS survey, according to which 73 to 75 percent of respondents believed that it should be completely impossible for foreign nationals to purchase forests, lakes, ponds, or other property with tourist attractions (Koblanski, 1996).

Historically, Polls and Russians do not see each other very favorably, despite long years of coexistence and fruitful economic cooperation. The countries were engaged in several wars against each other. Poland was part of Czarist Russia. After World War II, Poland's independence was severely limited and the country became its big Eastern "brother's" satellite. Until the early 1990s, Soviet troops were stationed on the Polish territory. Soviet dominance could also be felt in Polish education and culture. During the last year of the Soviet Union, as many as 70 percent of Poles believed that the U.S.S.R. was the country Poland should fear most (in 1987, 12 percent of the people thought so and 24 percent suggested this in 1990). According to 61 percent of respondents in a 1991 survey taken by the CBOS opinion research center, Soviet policy constituted the "biggest threat" to world peace. Only 4 percent of the respondents perceived the U.S.S.R as an ally, compared to 46 percent in 1987 and 18 percent in 1990 (*Gazeta Wyborcza,* 1991, n. 49, February 27).

In 1993, 39 percent of Poles believed that in the next five to ten years Russia would try to restore its empire. In 1995, the number reached 64 percent. In addition, 58 percent of respondents said Russia, because of its plans to regain control over Poland, would object Poland's admission to NATO (Tretyakov, 1995). A 1994 CBOS poll showed that Poles increasingly believed Russia threatened Poland's sovereignty. More than half felt Russia aimed to dominate the countries of Eastern Europe as it did until the collapse of communism in 1989. Closely tied up with the new fear of Russia is disillusionment with the West—particularly the long-beloved United States. Some 58 percent of Poles expressed their concern that NATO was making deals with Russia about Poland behind its back (McKinsey, 1994). Political turbulences in Russia still echoed in Poland. In a 1994 survey, 70 percent of Poles said the events in Russia might endanger Polish security (UPI, 1994, January 21).

According to a 1995 CBOS survey, 72 percent of Poles believed that in the near future Russia would try to regain the former Soviet Union's influence in Eastern and Central Europe. In 1993, the same concern was shared by only 39 percent of people. Among the main reasons for these concerns, which could have influenced the results of the poll, was Moscow's opposition to the expansion of NATO and Moscow's strengthening links with Belarus, which was commonly viewed as a threatening act against Poland (PAP, 1995, July 31). Another survey by the CBOS polling center conducted on a national adult sample of 1,101 people in 1997 revealed that 43 percent of Poles believed that the proposed unification of

Russia and Belarus might threaten Poland's interests (PAP, 1997, February 18). Overall, 27 percent of Poles believed in 1999 that Poland's independence was threatened. According to the CBOS, fear of losing independence in some people stemmed from their perceptions of the Balkan conflict and the active role Russia tried to play in it (PAP, 1999, June 10).

Poland is a country with a relatively small proportion of minorities,[2] and many citizens—even though they significantly overestimate the amount of different ethnic and religious groups in the country[3]—want to keep their nation homogeneous. For instance, in a poll run by the CBOS, 58 percent of the population expressed their support for a more restrictive border-control system. The restriction supporters explained their standpoint with the need for more security and protection against migrants from the east (PAP, 1998, March 10).

However, in general, Poles are feeling increasingly secure. In 1991, 44 percent of Poles believed in an external threat to Poland and in 1996 only 27 percent. Also, in 1994 only 32 percent of Poles believed that the West would help Poland during a conflict and in 1997 this belief was expressed by 58 percent of Poles (*Gazeta Wyborcza,* 1997, n. 199, August 27). Only 4 percent were concerned about a military conflict with a neighboring country (*Gazeta Wyborcza,* 1996, n. 55, March 5). About 53 percent voiced the opposite opinion when asked by the CBOS polling center about the situation of Poland on the international arena (PAP, 1999, June 10).

Concluding Remarks

After more than 10 years of political, social, and psychological transformation, most Polish people believe that the foundations for a democratic system have been laid. Basic economic and institutional reforms have been carried out. After the initial political chaos, the sociopolitical situation in the new millennium is becoming stable. Politicians and voters learn more about democracy. People learn how to cope with many unwelcome developments that may occur in their country, such as unemployment and widening social polarization (Czapinski, 2000). People also adjust to the new social system and continue to learn how to rid themselves of some of their unrealistic expectations and fears.

Notes

1. Sometimes metaphors help to convey descriptions better. In 1998, Poles were asked to specify Poland's place in an imaginary, three-story common European house in the year 2000, in which the top floor is posh and luxurious, the first floor offers average comfort, while the ground

floor contains low-standard apartments. Most respondents relegate Poland to the ground floor, together with Romania and Russia, and below Spain, Italy, Belgium, Czech Republic, and Hungary (*Polish News Bulletin,* July 31, 1998).

2. Poland is relatively homogenous in terms of its ethnicity and religion. Poland has almost 40 million inhabitants; more than 90 percent of them declare themselves Catholics (Grabowska, 1997). National minorities represent a small proportion of the population and includes Germans (500,000 –700,000), Ukrainians (300,000 - 400,000), Belarusians (250,000 - 300,000), Lithuanians (20,000 - 30,000), Slovaks (20,000 –25,000), Jews (5,000 –10,000). (*Gazeta Wyborcza,* September 14, 1999, p. 6; in Poland, no official records of ethnic minorities are kept, this is why the numbers quoted here are approximate.) There are relatively small groups of Romany, Greeks, Macedonians, Russians, and Tatars. Poland is bordered on the Baltic Sea in the north, and after political changes in the east it borders the Russian Federation, Lithuania, Byelorussia, and Ukraine. In the south, Poland borders Slovakia and the Czech Republic; Germany is adjacent to Poland from the west. The country's borders—mainly because they were established arbitrarily by the victorious powers of World War II—are still subject to discussion and territorial claims.
3. According to a CBOS public opinion poll taken in August 1999, Poles overestimated the size of ethnic minorities in Poland. In fact, only 3 to 4 percent of people were born outside of Poland. However, more than one third of the respondents put the total estimated number of immigrants at 10 percent of the population. Correct estimates of the number of national minorities were given by 35 percent of respondents, with 23 percent having no opinion (*Gazeta Wyborcza,* September 14, 1999, p. 6). An opinion poll in Poland, where there are fewer than 10,000 Jews, found that 25 percent of Poles believed there were between 750,000 and 3.5 million Jews in the country (Doyle, 1993).

Chapter 5

Ukraine: Fears and Uncertainty

Vladimir Paniotto and Eric Shiraev

Ukraine is one of the largest European countries with a population over 50 million people, 20 percent of whom are ethnic Russians. Similarly to other post-totalitarian countries, Ukraine went through a painful process of political, social, ideological, and economic transformation. There is a great variety of negative and positive symptoms of the transformation process that can be typically found in all post-communist societies. Economic problems, lack of democratic experience, a weak legal foundation of society, inadequate law enforcement, psychological resistance of the population to changing conditions, and many other factors affect social and political transformation in the majority of post-Soviet states.

In contrast, there are several specific conditions, including economic, political, and cultural, that altogether determine the relative uniqueness of Ukrainian experience. These conditions have a significant impact on most people's fears and worries. Among these circumstances are the lack of the country's own energy sources, relatively slow—compared to the neighboring Russia—process of radical economic transition, persistent territorial and economic disputes between Ukraine and Russia, especially over the Crimea peninsula, the status of Sevastopol port and its military base, and the division of the Black Sea fleet.

As was mentioned at the beginning of the chapter, Ukraine has a large ethnic Russian population. Other ethnic groups are much smaller, and proportions of each of them do not exceed one percent. One specific element of the Ukrainian experience is that the country is historically divided into at least three large sections: central, southern, and western regions. Their demographic and ethnic composition varies due to many socioeconomic, political, cultural, and religious circumstances that influenced the contemporary development of the country and the formation of the Ukrainian nation.

During the first ten years of post-Soviet development, in national surveys Ukrainians expressed a great variety of politically and ideologically diverse attitudes. An opinion poll of a national sample of 3,082 individuals conducted in 1996 by a research team at the Social Monitoring Centre (a unit of the National Institute of Strategic Studies in Kiev) revealed that among Ukrainians, 17 percent referred to themselves as being on the "left" end of the ideological spectrum, 10 percent said they were on the "right," and 18 percent called themselves "centrists."[1] More than 55 percent of respondents did not identify their political affiliation (Salabaj and Yaremenko, 1996).

Lack of Confidence in the Future

The individual's fears tend to grow in the situation of uncertainty. Uncertainty in one's life may be affected by this person's lack of trust in and weak support of the existing social and political system. By the mid-1990s, in Ukraine—similarly to Russia and Belarus—such support for the new political system was averaging 30 percent, approximately twice as low as the level of support in countries such the Czech Republic, Slovakia, Hungary, Poland, Slovenia, Bulgaria, and Romania (Rose, 1996). It is likely that the level of trust should determine the individuals' confidence in the future. The lower the trust is the lower the person's degree of confidence in the future. The less someone is confident of the future, the more troubles he or she should anticipate. For the Ukrainian people, the degree of such confidence was distributed as shown below in table 5. 1.

As you can see from the table, two thirds of Ukrainians expressed an obvious lack of confidence in their future. More than four out of ten people said that they were absolutely not confident. Most people associated the word "future" with their own personal life. For example, clarifying the respondents' meaning of the word future, 71 percent of the interviewed had in mind both themselves and their families. A relatively small number of respondents—15 percent—were assessing their confidence in either the whole country's future, the future of humankind, or the entire world.

There are certain group-related differences found in the expression of confidence. Among the youngest age cohort—people aged between 18 and 29—almost 10 percent were entirely confident of their future, while 35 percent were not certain about it at all, which is slightly lower than in the general sample. Middle-aged adults expressed their confidence at the level similar to the general sample. Among the people of the senior age co-

Table 5.1 How Confident Are You in Your Future? (in percentages). Source: "Catastrophic Thinking in the Modern World." Year: 1998[2]

Absolutely confident	8
Very much confident	14
Very much not confident	22
Absolutely not confident	42
Difficult to say	14

hort (55 and older), 47 percent expressed no confidence about the future, which is slightly higher than the national average.

To give a more detailed interpretation of the results, let us introduce a simple statistical quotient that indicates a ratio between those individuals who are absolutely lacking confidence in their future (we will call them pessimists) and those who have absolute confidence (optimists). If the quotient for a particular sample is "1," this means that the sample contains equal amounts of pessimists and optimists. The higher the quotient, the more pessimists are in the sample. Overall in the Ukrainian national sample the "pessimism" quotient was 5.25, which means that pessimists outnumbered optimists with a ratio of more than five to one. This quotient for the youngest age cohort was 3.5 and for the senior cohort it was close to 6.

The tendency to perceive the future in an optimistic, fear-free way is, perhaps, what one should expect from younger generations, compared to older age groups. However, neither psychologists (Erikson, 1968; Levinson, 1978), nor political scientists (Sigel, 1989) believe that this tendency is universal. There is no compelling empirical evidence that would suggest that the individual's subjective feelings of optimism or pessimism should correlate with his or her age. There are many social, ideological, and political conditions that mediate the development of the individual's particular perceptions about the future. Specifically in the Ukrainian case, from the beginning of the societal transformation people had to adjust to many new rules of new society, cope with lowering living standards—at least for most of people—and most importantly, accept the growing number of uncertainties in their lives. Many of those individuals who learned how to be successful in the old Soviet social system find the adjustment process extremely difficult. On the other hand, those people whose socialization was taking place in a new and changing society may have better chances to adjust because they did not have to give up many of their previously formed attitudes and habits. Maybe for this reason somewhat less pessimism is found in the young in comparison with more mature categories.

Another factor may also significantly contribute to many senior adults' worries and feelings of uncertainty. The Ukrainian government, which initially established a goal to maintain its policy of social protection of the elderly, began to shift its priorities. Due to serious financial constraints, the government revised the overall social security policies and took other steps that gave the seniors many new reasons to be more anxious and pessimistic than other generational groups. Older people in the country were facing a gradual decline in the quality and quantity of social security programs. They had more difficulties finding jobs suitable to their qualifications. In addition, many of them were lacking specific skills that were necessary in contemporary business enterprises, such as foreign language skills and computer proficiency. Age discrimination in hiring and firing made older Ukrainians especially vulnerable: The government could do very little to guarantee protection to the worker against age discrimination.

There are also gender-related differences in the expression of respondent's certainty in their future. Among the surveyed men, there are 11 percent of optimists and 39 percent who expressed very pessimistic views. Among female respondents, there are 6 percent of optimists and 44 percent of pessimists. The pessimism quotient yields solid evidence of the attitudinal gender gap: it is 3.5 in men and 7.7 in women. Compared to men, there are more Ukrainian women who, overall, maintain pessimistic views about the future. Among a great variety of factors that can affect the gender gap in attitudes, socioeconomic conditions may play an increasingly important role. Even though Ukraine is a democratic state, women may find it is more difficult, compared to men, to succeed in the capitalist system that lacks many essential elements of social protection.

The only group that expressed a majority of optimistic opinions was one of small-business entrepreneurs. Conceivably, successful business-related activities and development of entrepreneurial skills can provide the individual with a greater sense of control, satisfaction, and, eventually, hope. Another group—college students—contained approximately equal proportions of optimists and pessimists. The highest proportions of those who express no-confidence attitudes about their future are found among the unemployed and the retirees.

Educational level of respondents and confidence in the future are also linked. People with college degrees turned out to be less pessimistic than those with only high-school diplomas. People with higher incomes were also found to express more optimistic attitudes than those who made less money. For example, for those who were making 300 *grivnias* per month, the index of pessimism was .50. For those making between 200–300 *grivnias* a month, the quotient was zero. Such an innate reality of capitalism that links personal feelings, including self-assessment of well-being, to money is not new to Ukrainians. Even in a socialist society, the amount of money in one's possession could have determined an individual's social status and his or her access to other resources. What changed in the 1990s was that money became an important measure of survival. No longer could one be promised social protection, which was guaranteed during the years of socialism. As in other national cases described in this book, economic worries during the transformation period were among the most serious concerns of Ukrainian people.

Economic Concerns

Economical conditions in Ukraine during the transformation period were characterized by an essential decline of production during the period from 1991 to 1996. The country's GDP dropped 52 percent over the first five years of independence. In the late 1990s the decline had slowed down and the economy began to show signs of improvement.[3] One of the many noticeable demographic developments that affected the country's economy and its overall development was depopulation. From 1990 to 1996 the share of population engaged in all spheres of economic activities was reduced by almost 9 percent. Moreover, from 1991, death rates repeatedly exceeded birth rates (Statistical Yearbook of Ukraine, 1997). According to the results of the sample survey conducted by the State Committee of Statistics, the employment level of population from ages 15- to 70-years-old was 64 percent (October, 1996), which was significantly less than in the pre-crisis period.

As in most post-Soviet countries, economic problems were the most serious causes of worries for the vast majority of Ukrainians. In the 1990s the living standards of about half of the population of Ukraine were below the subsistence level. According to a survey of 4,500 people conducted by the Kiev International Institute of Sociology, the salaries of half of the country's households were below the cost of the consumer basket. Only 5 percent of the polled indicated that their financial situation was stable (ITAR-TASS, October 1, 1998). Among the issues that worried people most, low income was the most salient problem. It was mentioned by the overwhelming majority of the respondents: 93 percent replied that they were either somewhat worried or worried very much about their lack of money. More people expressed their concerns about money than they did about their health.

Lack of housing—one of many social problems inherited from the Soviet era—was mentioned as a source of worry by 53 percent of people. Living conditions are traditionally one of the most persistent problems inherited from the Soviet times. For decades, bureaucracy in Kiev and officials in local governments were responsible for the construction and distribution of apartments, particularly in urban areas. As in most places in the Soviet Union, citizens were prohibited from having individually owned dwellings in the cities. Worries about living conditions are positively correlated with the respondents' age: Older Ukrainians, due to their financial situation and social status, had fewer chances than younger groups to receive a new apartment from the government or buy one on the market.

Not only people with small incomes mentioned concerns about the amount of money they were making. Similarly, those people who described their financial situation as average or great also expressed monetary concerns. For example, 88 percent of those who perceived their material status as "average" worried about their income: It was perceived as low compared to other people. Among those Ukrainians who reported higher than average and high incomes, money was a concern for 63 and 40 percent respectively (Salabaj and Yaremenko, 1996).

The extrapolation of existing negative perceptions of society and economy—including people's own assessments of their finances and living conditions—upon something that did not happen as of yet may explain why there are so many people in Ukraine in the new millennium with a gloomy outlook on their future. The continuing economic difficulties in Ukraine perhaps influenced people's imagination and made their pessimistic attitudes easily accessible. In a way, it was a rational assessment of their present: Many people had very few options other than to imagine that the future of the country would be as gloomy as its state after ten years of transformation.

One out of every two citizens of Ukraine—52 percent—believed that the division between the rich and the poor is unjust, while significantly fewer people—31 percent—believed that inequality is natural for society. There is perhaps no single explanation of why many Ukrainians are apprehensive about the major market-driven principles of government and distribution of resources. On the one hand, it could be a result of a socialization process: Millions of people in contemporary Ukraine grew up in a socialist country. A safety net that socialist society offered to its members created in many people a special feeling of entitlement: Even though one person is more successful than the other, government should take care of this situation, so that no one advances too far. Beliefs in social equity continued to be a major influencing factor of the Ukrainian public opinion. However, on the other hand there is a legitimate human inclination to choose safety and security over risk and uncertainty. Forty-eight percent of people said that they would prefer to live in a country in which the government regulates the economy and establishes retail prices and wages than in a free-market society. Additionally, 59 percent of respondents preferred to live under the government that guarantees a certain standard of living to every citizen (Salabaj and Yaremenko, 1996).

The high level of poverty in Ukraine is one of the main obstacles to the implementation of decisive and meaningful economic reforms, which require the restructuring of production, reorientation of investments, and the closing of unprofitable enterprises. This requires human mobility, determination of political leadership, and new managerial skills. In addition, people have to trust the government. However, in Ukraine, people's level of trust in the regime was thinning during the 1990s. Partly because of people's concerns and worries about their future, millions of Ukrainians voted for communist candidates in local, parliamentary, and presidential elections.[4] And their choice was not necessarily a reflection of their ideological views. Many people voted counting on their personal security and social protection, promised to them by the left.

In general, according to surveys conducted for this project the distribution of Ukrainian people's opinions about socioeconomic issues resemble many attitudes expressed by people in neighboring Russia. Nevertheless, the level of worries in Ukraine was somewhat greater than in Russia. Ukrainians were more concerned, compared to Russians, about "impoverishment"—87 percent against 71 percent in Russia; and "mass unemployment"—78 percent compared to 60 percent in Russia.

Foreign Threats

Government's relentless arguments about the dangers of "capitalist encirclement," constant search for foreign spies and domestic traitors, were essential elements of Soviet-style Cold War propaganda. Due to the absence of legitimate opinion polls, it is difficult to give empirical accounts of what Ukrainians felt about foreign threats during the Soviet times. First surveys on this issue were taken in a new geopolitical situation. Ukraine gained its independence. Former neighboring republics became sovereign states. On the western border, Hungary became a member of NATO, an alliance that for decades was considered by millions of Soviet citizens as aggressive and expansionist. From the northern and eastern borders, some Russian politicians continued to make territorial claims to some territories in Ukraine. How did Ukrainians begin to perceive foreign threats to their country?

First and foremost, the main source of concerns and worries for most Ukrainians since gaining independence was not the West but Russia. Although the Russian government could not effectively influence Ukrainian domestic politics, Russia had many economic and political tools to do so. Furthermore, over the years of independence Russian people's attitudes toward Ukraine and Ukrainians have been rather controversial. These developments sparked additional worries in many people in Ukraine. On one hand, the majority of Russians hardly saw the neighboring Ukraine as either enemy or adversary. According to the All-Russian Public Opinion Research Center in November 1997, while 22 percent of Russians professed "absolute trust" in Ukrainians, 61 percent said they regard them "calmly, without any concern." Only 1 percent of the surveyed Russian admitted they view Ukrainians with "fear," and 5 percent with "irritation and distrust" (*Ogonyok,* February 1998).

On the other hand, regarding a wide range of social and political issues related to the countries' bilateral relations, Russian public attitudes were not necessarily forthcoming. According to a 1997 poll conducted by the All-Russian Public Opinion Research Center, 33 percent of Russians did not like the idea of granting permissions to so-called guest workers from neighboring states to work in Russia, including Ukraine—that in the 1990s already had thousands of individuals working temporarily in hundreds of Russian businesses and enterprises. Only 25 percent of the interviewed supported this idea about foreign workers (*Segodnya,* June 2, 1997). Over 60 percent of Russians have always viewed the two independent countries as one state. A total of 62 percent of Russians would like Ukraine to join the union between Belarus and Russia (Panshina, 1998). The view that Russia should own Sevastopol was supported by 78 percent of the interviewed (Interfax, February 26, 1999). In addition, 41 percent of Russian people considered the policy of the Ukrainian government not friendly toward Russia (Public Opinion Foundation [Obshestvennoe mnenie], October 25, 1999). This ambivalence of Russian respondents' attitudes, ranging from acceptance of Ukrainians as a people and individuals to supporting territorial claims against their country, moving from general friendliness to prejudice-based mistrust, can be alarming signs for millions of Ukrainians, which, in turn, influence people's opinions about Russia and the Russian people as a group.

Attitudes of Ukrainians toward Russia and Russian-Ukrainian issues varied. For example, a 1997 opinion poll of the Ukrainian political elite revealed that the vast majority disagreed with the Russian territorial aspirations and claims. More than 50 percent of the interviewees expressed the opinion that the Russian Navy should not be allowed to stay in Sevastopol for more than ten years. About 10 percent agreed to the Russian presence in the city for a period of more than ten years and 11 percent demanded the navy's immediate withdrawal (Kapustin, 1997). At the same time, according to a 1998 national poll held by the Democratic Initiatives fund and the Sotsis-Gallup firm, 57 percent of voters in Ukraine were ready to back a candidate for the Ukrainian parliament or a political party or a bloc that he or she represents if they defend the idea of Ukraine's admission to the Russia-Byelorussia union (see chapter on Belarus). An impressive proportion of people—44 percent of respondents—favored granting the Russian language the status of a second state language in Ukraine (Melnik, 1998).[5]

With the ending of the Cold War and the disappearance of the image of a "legitimate" foreign enemy, the role played by the United States and NATO, people's fears about foreign invasion have been significantly reduced. Moreover, the fact that Ukraine no longer is a communist country, its ruling elites embraced the idea of partnership with the West, and some politicians and numerous nongovernment experts began to discuss the idea of Ukraine's integration into NATO and the European Union. Public support of economic integration with the West was strong: Polls showed that 79 percent of the country's population supported Ukrainian membership of the EU (*Holos Ukrayiny,* 1999). "Americanization of life" troubled Ukrainians less than it did Russians (18 percent against 27 percent).

People's reaction to the tragic events of September 11 was similar to the reactions in other countries in the region. On September 12 and 13 (2001) VTsIOM conducted a poll of 400 Kiev residents. (A similar poll was conducted in Moscow). The terrorist attacks primarily aroused indignation in 75 percent of respondents. In Kiev, 15 percent of respondents mentioned feeling fear. In Kiev, 50 percent of respondents considered other terrorist attacks possible in other countries. Along with this, 54 percent said that the September 2001 terrorist attacks might lead to beginning of a new world war.

Popular support of the idea of Ukraine joining NATO was substantial but not overwhelming. It even dropped slightly over the course of the 1990s. For instance, in 1993, 48 percent of the Ukrainians wanted to see their country as a NATO member. In comparison, only 37 percent of people in 1997 share the similar view (Batyrsky, 1997). It is unclear how many people did not like the idea about the alliance because of their ideological and political beliefs and what proportion of the population based their opinions on xenophobic fears and anti-Western emotional outbursts. What is important in the context of these polls is that the reluctant approach of many Ukrainians to be embraced by NATO and serious concerns about a possible Russian retaliatory actions if Ukraine attempts to join NATO were mentioned among several reasons for why the government in Kiev did not actively push for political integration with the West (Khandohiy, 2000).

Respondents' ethnicity should be taken into account whenever attitudes about bilateral relations are analyzed. In 1996, overall, about 30 percent of respondents expressed their worries about the relationship between

Russia and Ukraine (Salabaj and Yaremenko, 1996). However, among Russians, the number of people who expressed their worries was 42 percent. There were significantly fewer indications of concern among Ukrainians; only 25 percent expressed their anxiety. Older people are also more concerned than the young. Only 14 percent of respondents aged 18 to 19 expressed their concern about Russian-Ukrainian relations, while 35 percent of the 50 to 59 age group were concerned. There were also territorial differences in attitudes about this issue. The largest percentage of people worried about the current relationship between Russia and Ukraine was found in the regions that are heavily populated by ethnic Russians. On the contrary western regions, in which ethnic Russians are a distinct minority group, expressed significantly fewer concerns. To illustrate, the following regions—Harkiv (45 percent), Donetsk (44), Dnipropetrovsk (41) and Odessa (41), as well as in Crimea (41 percent)—are ones with largest proportions of ethnic Russians. In the following regions, however, with the smallest ratio of ethnic Russians, the rates were much lower: Hmelnitsk (20 percent), Cherkassy (11), Rivno (10), Ivano-Frankovsk (7) and Ternopol (6) (Salabaj and Yaremenko, 1996).

According to a poll conducted by the All-Russian Public Opinion Research Center in November of 1997, 56 percent of Russians continued to regard Russians and Ukrainians as a single people, six years after the Byelovezh agreement that effectively separated Russia and Ukraine and dissolved the Soviet Union. However, more than half of all Russians considered relations between Moscow and Kiev to be "cold," "tense," or "hostile," while only 23 percent considered them "friendly," "neighborly," and "rather warm." Some 22 percent of the respondents considered the relations between the countries to be "neutral" (*Ogonyok,* February 1998).

Radiation-Related Concerns

After 1986, residents of Ukraine and neighboring regions of Russia and Belarus got accustomed to daily radio announcements about the levels of radiation in the region. Public opinion in these countries—because of safety and health concerns—is no longer insensitive to the radiation problem, which was virtually ignored in the Soviet Union before the 1986 disaster at the Chernobyl nuclear power plant. As it will also be mentioned in the Belarus chapter, the Chernobyl accident had a series of devastating and profound effects on the lives of millions of people in several countries. As estimated for the 1990s, Chernobyl cost Ukraine approximately $1 billion a year in various expenses and payments. Every taxpayer and every business in the country paid the Chernobyl tax—a mandatory fee of up to 12 percent of their monetary income.

After the explosion of the nuclear reactor in 1986, a massive emission of cesium, measured 2 million *curie,* was released from the station. Of this amount, 30 percent spread into Russia, 23 percent was absorbed in Belarus. Ukraine received 18 percent. Other European countries received less than 5 percent each (Interfax-Ukraine, July 29, 1998). There is no measure to reflect the value of human lives lost due to this enormous dose of radiation. According to assessments, the explosion and fire took lives of 238 people, those who developed acute radiation symptoms at the scene of the accident. About nine times as many people died over a ten-year period from additional radiation-related illnesses. Other sources mention the number of victims is close to 8,000 (Interfax, April 11, 2000). In Ukraine alone there are 6,447 communities in the zone of mandatory resettlement and about 800 more in the zone of voluntary resettlement. Medical records of approximately 468 thousand people have been put in the Ukrainian national and military registers of victims for monitoring purposes (Kapelyushny, 1996).

In 2000, President Leonid Kuchma pledged to stop the nuclear reactor at the station before December 15, 2000. More than half of Ukrainian citizens—56 percent—expressed their opinion that the Chernobyl nuclear power plant must be shut down as soon as possible, according to a national opinion poll of 1,935 respondents conducted by the Kiev Institute of Sociology in the spring of 2000. Meanwhile, 28 percent of Ukrainians thought that the plant must continue working and 16 percent were undecided. Even though 92 percent of the respondents feared the Chernobyl nuclear plant might be polluting the atmosphere, some still implied that shutting down the reactor would bring more economic hardship to the country, including energy shortages, price increase, and unemployment of thousands of professionals who would lose their jobs due to the plant closure. As you can see from the data, for more than one-fourth of people in this country the impact of economic fears could be more significant and devastating than the fear of radioactive contamination (Interfax-Ukraine, 2000).

It was rather expected that the fear of chemical and radiation poisoning in Ukraine—the country that experienced the Chernobyl tragedy—ranked second among all the mentioned fears (it was placed after the fear of "impoverishment" and before the fear of "mass unemployment") and that the number of Ukrainians who feared radiation was much higher than the number of Russians (81 percent against 53 percent). In addition, other ecological fears spread among people in Ukraine to a greater extent than they did among Russians. For example, 61 percent of Ukrainians expected "natural disasters" against 25 percent of Russians; 67 percent of the Ukrainians feared a "catastrophic crop failure" compared to 32 percent in Russia.

Other Concerns

Although 42 percent of the respondents believed that social cataclysms such as revolutions and counter-revolutions are the most probable and dangerous developments that can happen in the future, most people expressed most of their concerns and worries about "personal" issues. As expected, health and health-care concerns top the list of worries of most Ukrainians. Issues such as "poor health," named by 72 percent of people, and "threats to my health," suggested by 56 percent, were sources of concerns. Personal burnout—a consequence of persistent stress—worried 60 percent of people. Worries about alcohol abuse by a family member and substance abuse-related problems were mentioned by 28 percent of the respondents (Salabaj and Yaremenko, 1996).

Similar to neighboring Russia, crime was a major source of worry for most Ukrainians during the decade of post-Soviet life. About 74 percent mentioned their worries about crime in their country. Seventy-nine percent of Ukrainians expressed fears of "complete lawlessness." These worries could have affected people's opinions about a wide variety of other issues, including popular support for the death penalty. Specialists suggest, for example, that one of the reasons why Ukraine is not ready to introduce a moratorium on the death penalty—established in most European countries—is the reluctant stance of the country's public opinion (DINAU, 1999). In many countries, including the United States, Japan, and Ukraine, substantial proportions of population consider death penalty a legitimate and appropriate punishment for the criminal convicted in serious crimes. Capital punishment is also viewed as an effective measure that deters crime, and, most importantly, as a serious measure that helps many people to feel somewhat "safer" and cope better with their worries about crime (Ellsworth and Gross, 1994).

More than half of the Ukrainian respondents in 1996 were worried about problems associated with getting an education. This could be related to the necessity for many adults to work, which makes the combining of both employment and education a very difficult process. On the other hand, one should not forget that in Ukraine, college education is highly competitive and not everyone who wishes to get a degree can actually become a student because of the tough entrance exams.

Among several specific worry-producing issues indicated in open-ended questions, respondents mentioned primarily economic ones, such as "high rent," "the desperate situation among old people," "increasing prices for public services," "alimony is too high," "no chance to educate my children," and "irregular salaries." Moral issues also became sources of worries, such as "increasing alcohol and drug use," "bad attitude towards pensioners and veterans of the Second World War," "the slow degradation of our society" (Salabaj and Yaremenko, 1996).

The study revealed an attitudinal tendency that was also established in other national samples (see chapters 3 and 4, for example): The younger generation tends to adjust to new circumstances better than older age groups do. Socioeconomic status and educational level also played a role in people's perceptions of threats and following reactions. For instance, the case of Chernobyl showed a particular trend: Poor people tended to ignore the disseminated information about the dangers of radiation. They did not move out the contaminated areas and even justified their inaction by suggesting that everything was all right. People with a higher education and socioeconomic status developed a more realistic image of the nuclear radiation dangers and were more informed about the consequences of exposure to radiation. The difference in attitudes between "higher" and "lower" social and educational strata is not only psychological. One group has more money, resources, and other opportunities than the other. As a result, some people fled the contaminated areas almost immediately after the accident, whereas others did not.

People's affiliation with political parties and interest groups also vary in the intensity of individuals' worries. Overall among people of the national sample, the stronger the opposition of the individual to the incumbent regime the stronger his or her worry-filled vision of the future. In Ukraine, for example, people who supported governing parties were likely to be more optimistic than other people; those who were in the opposition tended to be more pessimistic than others.

Concluding Remarks

Nearly 35 percent of Ukrainians strongly advocated a social order in the country backed up by authoritarian power (Melnik, 1998). It is quite possible that a substantial proportion of people—those who support authoritarian, non-democratic measures—expressed these attitudes because of their feelings of insecurity for their future. Therefore, many of them expect the government to interfere with the economy, control prices, pay guaranteed salaries, and provide for a certain standard of living for each individual. These expectations are symptoms of an authoritarian consciousness, which is a considerable obstacle to further democratic transformations.

Overall, almost 70 percent of the surveyed suggested that various calamities offered to the respondents for their assessment are possible and realistic. In 1999, more than 42 percent of the surveyed said they were not confident in their future. These results should not be surprising. The country's population, on one hand, is highly susceptible to extraordinary and unpleasant developments and "bad news," such as the Chernobyl disaster, coal mine explosions, and scandals within the government. On the other hand, if people have little chance to avoid social and ecological calamities, if they have little power to influence events around them, then pessimism and withdrawal can become prominent psychological features of many individuals. In both scenarios there will be particular political forces ready to manipulate public opinion and use this situation to achieve their political goals.

Notes

1. In the United States, for example, from 1960 to 2000 proportions of people who identify with the "center" or moderate views are much higher than in Ukraine; they vary over the period of observation, from 37 to 51 percent (Shiraev and Sobel, 2002).
2. This study is based on the research project "Catastrophic thinking in the modern world" (the "Catastrophes–98" project) conducted by the Kiev International Institute of Sociology.
3. In 1990 the decline was at the 4 percent level; in 1994 the decline accelerated and reached 23 percent to slow down by 1995 to 12 percent and in 1996 to 10 percent.
4. Ukrainian experience resembles one of many other ex-communist countries in which popular reform-oriented politicians were challenged by their political opponents from the "left." In the Ukrainian case, during the presidential elections President Leonid Kuchma sustained a challenge of his main rival, Peter Simonenko.
5. Some former Soviet republics began to reverse their one-language policy established in the early 1990s. For example, in 2000, Kirgyzstan restored the Russian language as the country's official second tongue.

Chapter 6

Belarus: Fears, Hopes, and Paradoxes of the Transformation

Larissa G. Titarenko

Populated by ten million people, Belarus—the former Byelorussia—is one of three "sister" countries, including Russia and Ukraine, which have much in common. They share related ethnic, linguistic, religious, and cultural roots. According to the results of the 1999 census, 81 percent of population are Belarusians, 11 percent are ethnic Russians, 4 percent claim Polish ethnicity, 2 percent are Ukrainians, and 0.3 percent are Jewish (Zinoskiy, 1999). For centuries, both the Russian Empire and the Soviet Union unified these countries politically and economically. Nevertheless, in the 1990s and afterwards, these three countries were transforming in quite dissimilar ways and with different speed.

Belarus, by the beginning of the millennium, appeared to be frozen in time. Almost any casual observer could have formed this impression. The streets in Minsk named after communist icons (Lenin Avenue, Marx Street, etc.) were not renamed, as it had happened in most capitals of the post-Soviet states. Red flags flew on flagstaffs during the traditional Soviet days of celebration in May and November. The security service in Belarus held the title of the KGB after ten years of the country's independence. The biggest national newspaper was still named *Soviet Byelorussia [Sovetskaya Byelorussia]*. By 2002, the scope of privatization in Belarus was insignificant, with practically only small cafes, shops, and street kiosks in private hands. Private industry was mostly limited to the service and trade sectors. A Soviet-style planned economy still prevailed in most areas. According to official data, in the beginning of the millennium, the state owned all but 20 percent of industry and businesses.

It is inaccurate to assume that nothing at all had changed in Belarus ten years after it broke with the Soviet Union. The "old" Communist Party was gone and people could vote in multi-candidate elections, travel, and express their opinions more freely than they could fifteen or twenty years ago. However, the elected president consolidated more power than previous communist leaders of the Soviet Byelorussia. Compared to 1991, people changed considerably: they were more frustrated, alienated, and critical of their life than ever before. The elevating spirit of the early days of *perestroika* had long gone. Fears returned. People's major concern was making sure that things did not get any worse under the constant pressure of unpredictable economic conditions. These are the symptoms suggestive of so-called catastrophic thinking (Shlapentokh and Matveeva, 1999).

Belarus after Independence

Several common factors have been affecting the transformation process in most post-Communist countries in Eastern Europe. Among these factors are the Soviet political legacy, ideological legacy of socialism, a wide range of cultural norms and values, the lack of market experience, and intricate economic problems. In this context, Belarus can be viewed as a "model case" that exemplifies a set of contradictory processes of the post-Communist transition, the events that are more or less typical for the vast majority of post-Soviet states.

From this point of view, one may expect that the fears and concerns of people in Belarus should be not much different from the worries of people in many other transitional East European societies. On the other hand, the picture of the social, economic, and political transition in Belarus, as it was mentioned earlier, displayed its own unique features. For example, governments in some former republic of the former Soviet Union chose an authoritarian line in their politics. In this sense, the country's political structure may resemble countries in the Caucasus region and central Asia, but not necessarily its Baltic neighbors, Russia, and Ukraine. Second, the appearing perspective of a new Belarus-Russia union—the development that had no other precedents in post-Soviet environment until the same process started in Moldova in 2001—received a relatively mild popular opposition compared to what the similar movement could have received in other countries. Historically in Belarus, anti-Russian sentiment and Russophobia were relatively weak and did not influence significantly the development of the country's governmental policies in 1992, right after Belarus gained its independence from the Soviet Union. In addition, partly because of its size (approximately the size of Kansas), lack of conflict-ridden ethnic problems, government control over the economy, and low level of economic privatization, the country had fewer problems such as inflation, organized crime, violence, terrorism, and threats of separatism compared to many other countries of the region. The price tag for such a relative social "stability" was the country's lack of reforms in economic and social spheres. Moreover, the living standards of the population were lower than the compatible parameters in the neighboring nations.

Quality of life: Major Worries

The deteriorating economic situation, the decline of the major standard of living, and the resulting impoverishment of the vast majority of individuals were among top worries expressed by people in Belarus over the first decade of this country's post-Soviet transition. In a comparative context, people's dissatisfaction with the present situation may be considered as a major characteristic of public opinion in Belarus and in several neighboring countries, including Ukraine and Russia (Ivanova and Shubkin, 1999). The countries differ, however, in the expressed extent of their dissatisfaction: it is lower in Belarus (approximately 50 to 60 percent of people who, according to different polls, express their disappointment), than in Russia (approximately 70 percent and higher), or Ukraine (higher than 80 percent) (Titarenko, 1999). Among those individuals who were satisfied with the situation in Belarus, 60 percent were over the age of 65, 38 percent assessed themselves as being of a moderate income level, and 33 percent were in the lower-than-moderate income bracket; 50 percent lived in villages or small towns. Among those who reported being fairly satisfied, 28 percent were older than 65. Among younger age cohorts, the satisfaction with the situation decreases. Even though the majority of Belarusians mention economic factors as a source of their disappointment, most people in surveys and on polling stations tended to support their president.[1]

Before the economic and political reforms started in the Soviet Union in 1985, Belarus was doing relatively well economically, compared to many other regions of the country. From the late 1980s, however, and especially after the collapse of USSR in 1991, the standards of living dropped drastically and continued an overall downward swing throughout the decade. The country's GDP fell sharply, from almost $4,000 per capita by the early 1990s to less than $1,000 in 1999. It is estimated that the standard of living in Belarus was four to five times lower than in Russia and roughly comparable to the standard of living in Ukraine (Eurasia Economic Outlook, 1999). The average monthly salary was approximately $40 in the beginning of the millennium (it was approximately $50 in Ukraine). Approximately one-third of the Belarus population in the 1990s lived below the official poverty line. The number of the poor increased and reached an 83 percent mark by the end of the 1990s. Due to low birth rates, high mortality rates, and continuous emigration, the country's population was decreasing at the rate of 30,000 per year (Tyavlovskiy, 1999).

As it was suggested earlier, and national surveys, in general, support this assumption, people's major concerns and fears were largely related to the economic sphere. The average individual was afraid that his or her standard of living could deteriorate further. According to the 1999 IFES survey, economic issues were mentioned as a major problem by 58 percent; 13 percent suggested social problems; and 5 percent mentioned political problems (Titarenko, 1999). On the other hand, the economic situation was relatively stable and not everything was gloomy and threatening in the perceptions of the economic sphere. Surveys also show a tendency of positive assessments of the economic well-being. Thus, in line with the data provided by the Center of Political and Social Research, the evaluation of the economic situation during the 1990s showed some improvement (table 6.1.)

By the end of the 1990s, Belarusians reported a higher level of satisfaction with the current state of affairs than did people in the neighboring countries. For example, the opinion gap between Belarusians and Ukrainians—in a country in which only 2 percent of people expressed their satisfaction—was 24 percentage points.

One of the factors contributing to the somewhat favorable perception of economic conditions in Belarus is the issue of wages. A crucial element of this country's economy is that the government pays most people's salaries. Only 10 percent of Belarusians reported that they were owed back wages, whereas in Russia and Ukraine such delays with payments were common and persistent during an entire decade. As measures aimed at slowing down inflation and stabilizing finances, non-payment and delays, for instance, were considered by Russian people as the most devastating problem facing their country in the 1990s. Ukrainian respondents reported that the issue of irregular payments (27 percent of popular support) was among major reasons of citizens' dissatisfaction with their economic situation (Ferguson, 1999). Many Belarusians were aware of a difficult situation with wages in the neighboring regions, and this could have affected their relatively favorable evaluation of their own situation. If this assumption is correct, it may partially explain why, unlike Russian and especially Ukrainian workers, the majority of Belarusian workers tolerated low wages and generally refrained from strikes and other political actions (Golovaha and Panina, 1999).

Perhaps some signs of possible improvement, coupled with a sense of relative stability, made some Belarusians express more positive opinions about their country than did people in Russia and Ukraine. According to

Table 6.1 Assessments of Changes of the Economic Situation in Belarus Compared to the Previous Year (Percentages). Source: Social, Political and Economic Situation in Republic of Belarus. Press-Release. Minsk. 1997.

Economic Situation	*1994*	*1995*	*1996*	*1997*
Became better	3	8	11	26
Remains the same	21	19	18	26
Became worse	61	72	64	37
Don't know	16	0	7	10

the 1999 USIA poll, three-quarters or even more people in Russia and Ukraine said things were going in the wrong direction; in Belarus 40 percent say things are going in the wrong direction compared to 39 percent who say things are going in the right direction. Overall, as it was mentioned earlier, most Belarusians did not have particular fears about unemployment or unpaid salaries. They were rather concerned about the further deterioration of their standards of living and eventual impoverishment.

Most of the time, such a "double vision" of the current situation contributed to a mixed self-perception of people's own financial situation. Even though many people were appeased by the current state of affairs, it did not eliminate their worries about the economic situation in the future. These fears—also known as economic fears—were noticeable in Belarus, especially during the early stages of the country's transition. Overall, only 15 percent believed that their family would be better off one year from the time of the survey in 1999; 28 percent believed their family's situation would be the same. A majority—more than 35 percent—expressed their concerns and anxiety that their family's financial situation would be worse.

Economic fears can be associated with and may be derived from the individual's lack of confidence in what is going on around him or her. These fears are also attached to people's lack of confidence in their current jobs, lack of hope of finding a better job, worries about inability to purchase what the individual considers important for his or her well-being, such as prescription medications or medical procedures. This type of fear was not present in the vast majority of people during the Soviet days for a seemingly obvious reason: the socialist state guaranteed a particular level of material comfort for every individual (although this level was very low). The state provided people with a dosage of psychological certainty about the future, reinforced by the benefits of free education, health care, and guaranteed pensions. Social conditions changed dramatically in the 1990s and left millions of people unprepared for the global transition in their lives.

Similarly to what was happening in Russia, millions of people in Belarus did not or could not successfully adjust to the growing uncertainty in their lives. Coupled with the realization that there are not so many ways to change society around them, this psychological uncertainty resulted in many individuals' behavioral withdrawal, emotional indifference, and social passivity.[2]

Domestic Worries: Politics and Government

Persistently, through the 1990s—and especially after Vladimir Lukashenko was elected president—Belarus was treated by experts and the Western media as a country with an authoritarian government. The paradox of transitional societies is that authoritarian and undemocratic governments—which, according to the observer's expectations, should quickly collapse as a result of the public opposition—in fact, find a strong backing across various social groups. Belarus is a fine example of this type of social and political development. Although Belarusians were not satisfied with many things in their lives, they, according to the mentioned already survey by USIA, (1999) had several issues that were viewed positively by the majority. For example, 83 percent of people said the government was doing a good job of ensuring timely payment of wages and pensions; 60 percent, indicated the government was doing a good job in public education; 55 percent, believed the authorities in Minsk were standing up for Belarus' interests in the world; and 54 percent confirmed their belief that the government ensures an adequate food supply for its citizens (USIA, 1999, July 22).

Even though that overall, citizens of Belarus tended to express diverse views on the emerging authoritarian political system, they also displayed a surprisingly high level of support for this system. On one hand, many people expressed their worries about the lack of democracy and violations of human rights. On the other hand, sizable proportions of people did not share such fears. To interpret these developments one should understand the nature of political processes in the country during the decade of its independence.

Lukashenko—a former state farm director—ousted Shushkevich—a Soviet-era apparatchik—in a surprise 1994 landslide victory. Likashenko presented himself as an outsider and defender of the common people. He was not particularly successful in his attempts to move the impoverished country away from the Soviet-era economic plans and social policies that have left it far behind the neighbors. Moreover, he did not appear to have intentions to do so. Despite the opposition's warnings and protests about the new president's authoritarian ambitions and actions, Lukashenko's popularity climbed up in 1996 to its highest level since his election in 1994. A constitutional referendum of 1996 extended the President's term for an additional five years and practically gave him control over the legislature, courts, and the country's media. Such strong popular support of Lukashenko was due to several factors, including, perhaps, his great populist skills, youthful charisma, and strong backing from conservative rural residents (Economist, 1996). By and large, he was one who could provide people with some sense of stability and assurances for the future. Hopes can reduce the individual's fears. Although there were fluctuations in public support, Belarusian president still had approval of a sizable proportion of voters by 2000 (Feduta, 2000)[3] and later.

Since 1994, Lukashenko's approval and popularity ratings did not fall below the 40 percent level (Vardomatsky, 1999). Moreover, in the IFES survey, 57 percent of the respondents said that they would vote to re-elect President Lukashenko again in the 2001 elections. Even though 17 percent were undecided about their choice and many people could have expressed their support in favor of Lukashenko because of their fear of persecution for expressing "anti-government" attitudes, opinion polls taken in the 1990s were relatively accurate predictors of electoral outcomes in Belarus.

Worries of European experts and politicians about a dictatorship and their appeals to Belarusians to change their mind have been persistent after Lukashenko took office. A major European newspaper came out with a headline: "All Power to Europe's Dictator; Vote in Belarus Kills Democracy" (Reeves, 1996). Fears that Belarus was sliding further toward an autocratic rule were expressed by Western politicians and numerous homegrown political watchdogs in Minsk (Van Der Laan, 1996). Javier Solana, the European Union's foreign policy chief, had told Alexander Lukashenko that unless he introduces democratic reforms, Belarus would face exclusion from the family of EU nations (Clover and Hargreaves, 2000). However, the average Belarusian remained practically undaunted about his or her choice of the leader. The majority of the population remained unmoved by the warnings about authoritarianism and maintained their support for a strong leader who would guarantee and provide security, and bring some stability to society.

Longing for societal stability and order is not a unique feature of public opinion in post-authoritarian countries. We find such patterns of public opinion in other places. The electoral successes of Violeta Chamorro in Nicaragua and General Lebed in Russia, popular support of authoritarian measures in the former Soviet Republics such as Georgia and Uzbekistan, and legislative victory of Communists in Moldova perhaps exemplify something that some observers of democratic transition overlooked or underestimated—substantial proportions of voters can be turned out by democratic slogans so long as these appeals do not provide to the people immediate material gains and benefits.

Among such benefits are safety and security of the nation and its inhabitants. Polls conducted in Belarus show that many people sincerely supported Lukashenko as a "father" of the nation (*bat'ka*), a person who understands, cares, and is capable of addressing people's needs. Several generations of people who have lived under socialism and developed an attitude of dependency on the government are likely to be resentful toward democratic changes and free-market transitions. For most of these people, free market competition and the establishment of merit as a criterion for societal success are two extreme challenges with which they could hardly cope. What Lukashenko was given credit for is the establishment of social order, low unemployment, guaranteed salaries and pensions, and relatively low crime rates. Altogether, these realities provided many of his supporters with a sense of security and reduced their worries about today.[4] This is another paradox of the Belarusian post-communist transition: Societal developments such as growing authoritarianism, socialism, and the unification with Russia were not as disturbing for many people as the calls for democracy, and freedom, and against the regime of president Lukashenko.

Such a solid support of government and its actions may also affect other people's attitudes, especially those that are related to government's activities. For example, one of the people's worries related to government was corruption. In Belarus, nevertheless, these fears appear to be less pronounced than in Ukraine, Poland, and Russia. Compared to other countries, fewer people say that corruption is a widespread and serious problem. Both the USIA and IFES surveys provide information suggestive of the differences among these three countries (USIA, 1999, July 22). This assessment of people's views on corruption and its impact on society reflects particular societal and political realities: the authoritarian regime either reduces corruption or makes it less salient.

Under the Shadow of Chernobyl

In May of 2000, fourteen years after the Chernobyl nuclear accident, five Israeli diplomats in Minsk were called back to Israel for medical tests; the Israeli Embassy was temporarily closed amid widespread speculations of increased radioactivity in the region. The diplomats were resting in their homes within a few hours (*Agence France Presse,* 2000). Practically all people in the Soviet Republic of Belorussia during the first days of the disaster stayed where they were. Throughout these years, the vast majority of Belarusian population continued to live under a persistent threat of radiation caused by the major nuclear-reactor catastrophe in the nearby Ukrainian city Chernobyl that took place in 1986. As the USIA (1999) survey found, 59 percent of people were very concerned and 29 percent were fairly concerned that they or their family members would suffer significant health consequences as a result of the Chernobyl accident. Only 11 percent said that they did not worry at all.

The Chernobyl accident has had a profound effect on the lives of millions of people and became the most devastating ecological disaster since World War II. More than two thirds of all respondents (68 percent) said that they or their family members have suffered ill health or adverse effects from the radioactive fallout of 1986. In the Gomel region alone, the most contaminated district in the country, 87 percent of people say their health suffered substantially because of the nuclear accident.[5]

A six-year-long survey on the psychological effects of the Chernobyl nuclear power plant disaster on the population showed the number of complaints about frequent headaches, fatigue, apathy, and a lack of motivation among the locals in Gomel and Mogilev regions. In both of these areas, the resulting radioactive fallout was 2.5 times greater than in other areas. Researchers and physicians who worked in the contaminated areas pointed out that persistent worries about health contributed to many people's psychological problems, including phobias, hallucinations, and substance addictions (Sidyachko, 1992).

Fears related to the Chernobyl accident remained among the most salient in Belarus long after the protective concrete sarcophagus was built around the damaged nuclear reactor. Throughout these years, people learned enough about the possible dangerous consequences of the accident. Unfortunately, too little was done in the country to prevent these dangerous potentials from becoming reality. As professor Bandazevsky (1999), Rector of Medical Institute in Gomel, wrote, "all Belarus is late" to fight the consequences of the Chernobyl disaster: too many tings have been contaminated and too many people are in jeopardy as a direct result of the radiation.

Knowledge about dangers caused by radiation made people very pessimistic about their health. The spread of fear of contamination—also known as radiation phobia—was partially elevated by people's exposure to different kinds of information, from rumors to television reports, radio interviews, and newspaper editorials (Shavel, 1998). As a result of the social policy of *pereseleniye* (evacuation) from the radioactive zones, contaminated or already ill people from these "dead zones" began their new lives in all regions of Belarus. According to many eyewitness sources familiar with the situation in the country, it was very common to hear stories about new health problems generated by the victims in the aftermath of the nuclear disaster. Consequently, new fears have been spread among new groups of people. No one in Belarus felt safe from the deadly radiation and its delayed consequences.[6]

On top of these worries, many people expressed their lack of trust in the government's effort to address people's fears and effectively fight their health-related problems. (In fact, the health care industry in Belarus is under state control). Only 31 percent believed that the government was doing its best to protect people's health. As the number of people who need medical care grows, as well as the number of cases related to radiation illnesses, the proportion of those individuals who blame the government is also growing. They develop a crippling fear of falling ill and not being able to receive sufficient medical care (Titarenko, 1999). As it was noted earlier, government was getting support for its role in many areas of the country's life. Health and environment-related area is one major exception. The majority surveyed by USIA (1999) survey said that the government did a poor job in cleaning up pollution (62 percent), and providing medical care and medication (69 percent) to the population.

Various natural disasters that happen in Belarus almost every year—twisters, floods, and fires—are not perceived as dangerous for people as the man-made Chernobyl problem. Meanwhile, fears of health deterioration and an apocalyptic future for Belarus, as a consequence of the Chernobyl disaster, did not spark any serious social action. People did not form grassroots political movements and did not send powerful lobbyists to Minsk to fight for a better solution to the radiation-related problems. A yearly protest rally, called *Chernobylskiy Shlyakh,* was more of a show than a protest action designed to change policy (Martinovich, 1999). People's "down-to-earth" concerns about daily needs, wages, inflation, and pensions outweighed their worries about health deterioration, which is considered by many as an "inevitable evil" that is impossible to fight and overcome (Titarenko et al., 1998).

This attitude of relative passivity and tolerance is closely related to a set of beliefs surrounding problems such as accidents, epidemics (including AIDS and tuberculosis), and chronic diseases (such as alcoholism). For example, many people in the country were exposed to the information about lethal consequences of AIDS. There is easily accessible information about people suffering from HIV and AIDS in Belarus. However, according to a college-population survey, although students were well-informed about AIDS, they did not practice safe sex or use other measures to prevent themselves from contracting this deadly disease (Titarenko 1998). Despite the rapid proliferation of illegal drugs in Belarus, most people expressed little concern or worry about the alarming problem of drug abuse (Nikolaychuk, 1999). Overall, there is a widespread lack of attention, care, and concern among Belarusians of all age groups about their health.

Foreign Threats

In the mid-1990s Belarus, surrounded by five countries, was one of the most militarized territories in Europe, with a 100,000-strong army equipped by 18 SS-25 nuclear missiles inherited from the Soviet times (Trickey, 1996). A country that throughout history suffered numerous military invasions and lost one-quarter of its population during World War II, Belarus had no legitimate military threat and no real enemy during the years of independence. However, some surveys show that quite a sizable proportion of people held fears of foreign invasion. For example, a 1999 USIA survey revealed that 27 percent were somewhat concerned and 28 percent were very concerned about the possibility that "another country might attack Belarus in the next five years" (*Opinion Analysis,* August 4, 1999).

Analyzing the results of this survey, one should look at the time in which the survey was taken. Like in the neighboring Russia, both spring and summer of 1999 were marked by the unprecedented anti-American and anti-NATO media campaign supported by politicians, experts, and opinion leaders of practically all calibers and orientations (Shiraev and Zubok, 2001). Before the 1999 escalation of the conflict in Kosovo and prior to the bombings of Serbia, Belarusians were not expressing such worries about the West. In 1997, only 7 percent suggested that the United States might threaten Belarus and three percent mentioned such a threat from Russia.[7] However, mild fears and concerns were mixed with isolationist attitudes on Belarus's international involvements. For instance, in 1999 people overwhelmingly opposed an idea—circulated for some time in the media—about Yugoslavia joining the suggested Belarus-Russian confederation. Among the main reasons for such a reluctant view was the opposition to sending Belarusian soldiers as peacekeepers to Kosovo. The same concern existed about a possibility of sending soldiers to war-ridden Chechnya or any other "hot spots" on Russia's territory.

One of the most salient and significant problems that the country faced on the international fields was the issue of its unification with Russia. For both Russian government and Russian public opinion, the "Belarus issue" was the matter of neither top priority nor urgency. For a smaller Belarus, though, the unification dilemma was one of the most important issues with a plethora of potentially far-reaching consequences. Of course, both optimists and pessimists, as well as liberal democrats and Communists sharply disagreed on what the consequences of the proposed unification could be.

Pessimists and democrats, however, were in the minority. One of the most remarkable developments related to the unification issue was a relatively strong support on both sides of the border. As the Russian-Belarus

1997 survey showed, more than three quarters of the surveyed population supported integration in both countries, especially economic integration, which received more that 80 percent strong support (see *Sotis,* 1999). Most Russians—72 percent in 1999 and 65 percent in 1997 supported unification with Belarus, according to two polls conducted by the Public Opinion Foundation (Interfax, 1999).

Two major political forces in Belarus, Lukashenko and his backers on one hand and the opposition on the other, stressed the importance of the unification issue and drew different predictions for Belarus's future (Karbalevich, 1999; Dragohrust, 1999). One group promised stability and a prosperous economic life, the other—turning the unification issue into a source of fears—developed doomsday scenarios of the country's semicolonial existence under the Russian rule. They called the supporters of the unification "enemies of Belarus" (Sushkevich, 2000). The media readily disseminated the arguments of both sides. The supporters put forward and defended primarily economic reasons for the union, the opposition attempted to argue about the forthcoming loss of political independence and an inevitable military occupation of the country by the Russian forces. Some predicted that Belarusians would hate Moscow as much as other neighbors hate it, and all these reasons combined would stimulate emigration from Belarus—because people would try to escape from a new authoritarian state—and the new wave of Cold War would start (Dubrovin, 1999). The further the negotiations between Yeltsin and Lukashenko moved, the more persistent became doomsday predictions about the forthcoming "disappearance of Belarus" from the map of Europe (*PolitRu,* 1999). Appealing to the anti-Lukashenko opposition, some argued that the unification with Russia would reinforce the authoritarian regime in the Kremlin. In contrast, some Russian media sources—very popular among most of Belarus viewers—warned about potential NATO attacks against small and vulnerable Belarus—in the same way as NATO acted against Serbia—if Minsk attempted to keep distance from Russia.

Overall, however, as it was pointed out in the chapter, according to many surveys, there were more supporters of the unification than opponents. The already cited here USIA survey (August 4, 1999) found that three out of four Belarusians supported the union between Belarus and Russia. Even though 63 percent of Belarusians believed that, as a result of unification with Russia, terrorists might start their activities in Belarus (*Nezavisimaya Gazeta,* 1999), most people considered a new merger between two former Soviet republics as rather positive than negative development. The results of these surveys demonstrated one of the most remarkable public-opinion phenomena during the post-communist decade in Eastern Europe: People's separatist attitudes and calls for sovereignty were shut down by the majority of popular opinion supporting unification with a neighboring nation.

Among several reasons of why the majority of Belarusians supported the union between the two states, was the deep economic crisis in Belarus, the country that had only few natural resources and an underdeveloped consumer market. Belarusians hoped that Russia would send them oil, gas, and electricity for low prices and, in turn, Russia would buy Belarus' industrial products. Most of ordinary Russians also supported the proposed union, because—among other reasons—they did not consider other Slavic republics "foreign states" and were concerned about destroyed or interrupted economic and interpersonal contacts with their friends and relatives in Ukraine and Belarus. From their opinion, a union between Belarus and Russia should be a hope for both nations (VTsIOM, 1999). In 1999, over 30 percent of Belarusians expressed their support to the idea of having Alexander Lukashenko as the leader of a union with Russia (Nezavisimaya Gazeta, 1999).[8] Although during 2000 and 2001 surveys showed both increase and decrease of public support of the proposed union, there were several political steps taken in Moscow that clearly signaled that Belarus was now treated by Russia in a different, somewhat "friendlier" way, compared to other countries. One of such steps was Russia's withdrawal from the accord on visa-free travel between several countries of the Commonwealth of the Independent States. The first exception was made to Belarus (Novoprudsky, 2000).

Fear and Apprehension

One of the ways to cope with anxiety and fears is to avoid contact with the source of apprehension. In social-psychological terms, such avoidance may be called social inertia. This behavioral and attitudinal pattern is, in part, a result of the individual's socialization that was taking place under the socioeconomic system of socialism. Overall, through a variety of egalitarian policies, by giving out perks and benefits, governments in socialist countries created conditions under which people considered themselves entitled to receive benefits and have access to resources. "Free medicine," "free housing," or "free education," and a "guaranteed job" were considered "normal" and even mandatory for society to provide to its citizens. Being deprived of individual freedoms under socialism, people meanwhile enjoyed their economic rights. They, in general, had no experience about how to compete for jobs, customers, and personal benefits. The legacy of socialism weighed heavily on their shoulders. This legacy prevented many individuals from accepting new values of competition and personal responsibility, freedom of speech, and tolerance to others. For the same reason, perhaps, most Belarusians supported the unification with Russia because it might have freed them from their fear of uncertainty: for centuries, these two Slavic peoples lived together in one state and this was a "normal" state of affairs. Therefore it should be this way in the future.

The authoritarian regime established in the Soviet Union especially valued obedience to authority. Obedience and conformity to the group were promoted by the whole system of education and political socialization. People in the U.S.S.R. and, of course, in Belarus, as its former republic, knew well what was happening to those who thought differently and expressed his or her views freely. Fear of authorities existed prior to *perestroika,* and it returned to Belarus in the late 1990s. At times when oppositional leaders are detained and persecuted, people prefer to lay low and hope for better times; fear of government exists but is not articulated, at least by the majority.[9] On the other hand, one may even suggest that high support of the unification with Russia could have caused—at least in some people—their hopes to regain freedoms they have lost in Belarus.

Psychologically, Belarusians have been experiencing less dramatic changes than Russians and Ukrainians, and most polls showed that they were dissatisfied with the changes to a lesser extent that their counterparts in "bigger countries." Other fears, at least on this stage of the post-Soviet transformation process, including environmental concerns and worries about national sovereignty and ethnic identity, were attached to people's concerns about their socioeconomic status and well-being. A strong authoritarian rule may significantly reduce fears of economic instability and societal disorder; the only question is how long people will accept authoritarianism.

One of the psychological pillars that support authoritarianism is fear of failure and longing for "old good days," which became especially noticeable later in the 1990s. For instance, in 1991, 69 percent of people in Belarus said that the decision to eliminate the USSR was "correct." By 1995, the number of supporters dropped to 6 percent, whereas 68 percent said that the decision was "incorrect" (*Nezavisimaya Gazeta,* 1996, February 10.). Unfortunately, Russia's unforeseen financial crisis in August 1998, the country's slow economic recovery, its inability to solve ethnic conflicts, lack of real positive social changes in the neighboring countries, numerous natural and manmade disasters, such as the submarine *Kursk* tragedy, further expansion of NATO, could produce new fears. Whether authoritarianism cures the average individual of its fears, remains to be seen in Belarus, a country under transformation.

Notes

1. Four in ten said that President Lukashenko was the figure most likely to resolve the economic problems Belarus was facing in the upcoming years;

56 percent intended to vote for Lukashenko in the 2001 presidential elections, 26 percent were satisfied with the current situation, and almost a third of respondents said Belarus is a democracy (Titarenko, 1999).

2. On the other hand, there were reports that challenged these and other statements about social passivity of people in Belarus. For instance, the majority of 1,100 people polled—75 per cent—predicted that they would take part in the forthcoming elections (Belapan, 2000).
3. The most visible forms of protest against Lukashenko and his authoritarian government are rallies and manifestations. However, there were only few of such events and they drew support of only tens of thousands—considerably less than the opposition was hopeful for.
4. Surveys held to draw a profile of Lukashenko's supporters: over age 55; educated to only the primary (77 percent) or secondary (56 percent) level; from the low income groups (72 percent of the lowest economic group and 62 percent of the "lower than moderate" group); residents of rural areas, especially villages (66 percent) and small towns (63 percent); from the regions geographically close to Russia (Vitebsk, Gomel, and Mogilev region); supporters of a state-controlled economy (57 percent strong supporters and 80 percent those who fairly strongly support it); those who say "Belarus is a democracy" (78 percent).

   On the contrary, Lukashenko's opponents oppose him regardless of the economic situation in Belarus; those who think Belarus is not a democracy (51 percent); who are younger (72 percent of strong opponents are age 18 to 44, and a majority of those at least somewhat opposed are 18 to 54); university educated (42 percent) or with a university degree (45 percent); strongly (51 percent) or at least somewhat strongly (35 percent) oriented to the market economy; and residents of Minsk (42 percent).
5. Although geographically the Chernobyl nuclear station belongs to Ukraine, the territory of Belarus has been polluted to a larger extent than any other area in the region. Many people who used to live in the polluted area not far from Chernobyl have been evacuated in 1986 and later. This fact brought additional concerns to the rest of the population, because it was believed that the evacuees brought their belongings, which were contaminated with radioactive dust.
6. The author interviewed a number of people in Minsk who have never been exposed to radiation and lived in Chernobyl region. However, these people appeared to worry about their health to a greater extent than did those who actually lived in those "dirty zones."
7. To protest against NATO expansion, Lukashenko threatened to keep the country's nuclear arsenal in violation of the START-I accord, which implied that the weapons must be returned to Russia by the end of 1996. He told the Russian State Duma that Western governments were siding with his parliament against him because of his opposition to NATO expansion. However, the missiles were under control of the Russian military and could not be launched by the Belarusians (Trickey, 1996).
8. However, these opinions were expressed when the Russian president was Boris Yeltsin, a person who could hardly be identified as a source of hope

and inspiration for people in both countries. As soon as Vladimir Putin was introduced as the new Russian prime minister in 1999 and then elected president in 2000, this young and energetic leader gained popularity among many people in Belarus.

9. Among well-known examples of how political opposition was treated in the 1990s is the case of Viktor Gonchar, chairman of the country's electoral commission. In March 1999, he was stopped by the police and dragged out of his car. Sentenced to ten days in prison, Viktor Gonchar went on hunger strike.

Chapter 7

Lithuania: Transitional Fears after Independence

Vladas Gaidys

With an influx of foreign investments and a push of pro-reform politicians supported by sizable majorities of voters, Lithuania by the beginning of the millennium has drastically changed from its Soviet past. Compared to many other ex-Soviet states, Lithuania's economy and trade after more than a decade of reforms were developing steadily and living standards were gradually improving (Maheshwari and Robinson, 2000). After ten years of independence, Lithuania had a GDP of approximately $10.6 billion, an impressive indicator of the relative success achieved by a post-communist country with population of only 3.7 million people (Snoddy, 2000). The pre–World War II Lithuanian currency, the *litas,* was reintroduced in 1993, pegged to the U.S. dollar.

Lithuania after Independence

In the political arena, the country's transformation coincided with its push for independence and the creation of an entirely new state and democratic government. On the March 11, 1990, Lithuania's Parliament—headed by the popular leader for the country's independence, Vytautas Landsbergis—declared independence from the Soviet Union. A new Cabinet led by Prime Minister Kazimiera Prunskiene was appointed. After a traumatic violent confrontation with Moscow in 1991, Lithuania won international recognition and gained full membership into the United Nations. However in the Parliamentary elections of 1992 the right-wing movement "Sajudis" lost the majority of seats, and the leftist candidates won the legislative majority. In 1993, former First Secretary of the Communist Party Algirdas Brazauskas was elected President. His party—renamed the

Lithuanian Democratic Labor Party—succeeded for a number of reasons; one of them was a promise to protect people from economic hardship caused by the country's transition to capitalism (Tarm, 1996). However, the promise did not materialize and the party rapidly lost its popularity among voters. As a result, in the 1996 legislative elections the Homeland Union party, headed by Vytautas Landsbergis, came back and won 70 of the 137 Parliament seats, whereas the ex-Communists received only 12.[1]

Political and economic reforms were taking place in a relatively stable societal atmosphere. The "smoothness" of the Lithuanian transitional period may be a major feature of the average Lithuanian individual's experience, which in many ways is different from the experience of people in most countries of the ex-Soviet bloc. Nonetheless, in the post-Soviet world, most people of Lithuania, as well as two other Baltic countries—Latvia and Estonia—shared many similar attitudes. After almost 50 years of the Soviet military occupation and followed political and cultural domination, most Lithuanians have grown to identify their country not as "Eastern Europe" but rather a "Central European" region. Polls repeatedly show that the majorities supports the country's expected joining the European Union and NATO. Such opinions and attitudinal tendencies are not so salient in other countries, besides Latvia and Estonia—and perhaps for obvious reasons, including geographical, ideological, political, and religious ones.

Lithuanians, on the other hand, as well as millions of people in other transformational societies, had to cope with many unprecedented consequences of free-market reforms, the results of which have inevitably increased ideological polarization and social inequality in society. Millions of people lost most of their social security benefits, previously guaranteed by the state. People had to learn new principles of democratic government and free press. Moreover, the crash of the Soviet system was perceived by the majority of population as a victory, but for a sizeable part of Lithuania's population—mostly Russian-speaking or pro-Communist citizens—it was a defeat and a true social catastrophe.

Overall, fears and concerns of Lithuanians reflected their individual perceptions of the economic, social, and political transformation. Fears also reflect people's assessment of their personal role and success in the ongoing social processes. Which factors influenced the intensity of fears? What impact did fears have on political, social, and economic life in Lithuania?

General Confidence in the Future

History teaches that unless a societal transitional process brings quick and sizeable benefits to the population this process rarely becomes a spur for people's confidence in the present and future. Even though Lithuania's path of transformation was not as difficult as it was in Russia or Belarus, people's confidence in tomorrow was not on a particularly high level. About one in every six Lithuanians in 1999—17 percent—said they were "absolutely not confident" in the future. Another 36 percent said they were "very much not confident." Overall, according to people's answers, more than 53 percent of the Lithuanian population were not confident about their future. Only 6 percent of people replied that they were "absolutely confident" and another 22 percent said they felt "very much not confident." As you can see, people with low confidence outnumbered "the confidents" with a two to one ratio.

There were some noticeable differences among attitudes of various social and demographic groups sorted out according to age, education, income, area of residence, and political identification. The most confident was the youngest generation. The middle-aged expressed the least confidence. Other surveys show a similar pattern: The young are more satisfied with their economic situation and more optimistic about their future than other age groups. There are multiple causes of such attitudinal gaps between generations, including those causes that are based on socialization experiences of different age groups and age-related differences in the social adjustment process. Cross-nationally, many representatives of older generations have more problems than younger men and women in terms of their ability to cope with new and constantly changing social conditions of contemporary free-market society (Shiraev and Levy, 2001).

College degree may be a positive individual accomplishment that helps compete in a new market economy. In fact, 38 percent of college graduates in Lithuania were confident in the future (26 percent with high-school education). Moreover, computer literacy and knowledge of the English language or other foreign tongues have served as a major boost to the individual's confidence by making him or her more competitive on the job market. Higher salary is also positively correlated with higher confidence. One quarter of Lithuanians were making approximately $100 per month and more at the time when surveys were taken. This group expressed the highest level of confidence at 44 percent. The level of confidence is remarkably higher in big cities (43 percent) than it is in Lithuanian provinces (17 percent). There should be several factors contributing to such a confidence gap. Among them are educational, age-related, and income-related conditions. People in big cities are generally younger; they are more educated, and make more money than their compatriots from small towns and villages.

It is quite remarkable that attitudes about the future are associated with the person's political identification. For instance, supporters of right-wing parties were more confident (Conservatives—40 percent) compared to supporters of left-wing parties (Labor Democrats—24 percent). When this survey was conducted, political conservatism in Lithuania was gaining popular support, whereas social-democratic ideas were compromised in the minds of many Lithuanians by mistakes in policies and personal failures of the left-wing government. This trend, which, as we see, could be influenced by pure political reasons and particular developments in the country, was found in other surveys taken at earlier periods (Gaidys, 1996).

Comparing Lithuanians' opinions to the results of surveys taken in other countries, one tendency cannot be left unnoticed: Lithuanians are less confident in the future than people of other post-communist countries, with the exception of Hungary, whose people expressed the same level of confidence as Lithuanians (Gaidys, 1996). It seems to be a social paradox: The country is doing relatively well, nevertheless, its citizens are more pessimistic than in other less successful countries. One of the factors contributing to these differences may be the religious identity of the majority of the Lithuanian population. Lithuania is a predominantly Catholic country compared to Estonia, which has a largely Protestant population.[2] According to some experts (Czuma, 1993), the Catholic world-view is more pessimistic than the Protestant. Self-reliance and self-appreciation is less typical for a Catholic "way of thinking," while fatalism and the resulting pessimism are more common. Of course, there are more than plenty of individual differences and there are pessimistic Protestants and optimistic and confident Catholics. In addition, the individual's religiosity has roots formed by the person's early socialization and experiences as an adult. However, as far as this religion-based hypothesis goes, statistically there could be a difference between these two large religious groups—Catholics and Protestants—in terms of their perception of the societal transition.

Economic Fears: Unemployment and Impoverishment

Socialism guaranteed jobs for every adult citizen. It was a written Soviet law according to which the capable individual must work. Free market gave people a different kind of experience: It made people realize that if one loses a job it will be no longer government's responsibility to help find a new one. Fear of becoming unemployed became reality in many people's lives. Almost 53 percent of Lithuanians felt "strong anxiety and constant fear" related to unemployment. It is usually given the highest place on the "rating list" of problems that people try to solve. For example, according to a poll conducted by the Baltic Studies firm, the biggest problems for Lithuanians in 1999 were unemployment (63 percent supported this view), and the worsening of the living standards (45 percent). Approximately 22 percent gave a general answer: They named the economic crisis in the country their major source of concerns (Burbulis, 1999).

For most Lithuanians, the term "unemployment" did not mean complete loss of a job. The term also means partial employment, or a job that produces so little income that it becomes impossible to live on it. Only 17.5 percent of respondents mentioned that they got enough money from their main job (pension) and for 81 percent it was not enough. Not surprisingly, many serious concerns were expressed about poverty and hardship. Almost 52 percent of the surveyed said that "decline of general level of life, impoverishment" made them experience "strong anxiety and constant fear."

In the 1990s, individual incomes in Lithuania remained relatively low compared to other developed European countries or to the United States. Under such conditions, how were people in Lithuania able to pay their bills and support free-market reforms? After 1994, Lithuania's economy was developing steadily and individual incomes, in general, grew. One of the most popular sources of additional income was growing food from family plot—46 percent of Lithuanians mentioned this as a source of food. This source of additional resources was popular even in the capital Vilnius (17 percent), in other big cities (20 percent), and in provincial towns (49 percent.) Among other sources, 23 percent of professionals in the country reported having an additional job.

Signs of Xenophobia

Lithuania, as well as every European country, is home to many ethnic groups. The two largest in this country are ethnic Lithuanians and Russians. The empirical data collected in this study revealed a relatively low level of xenophobic concerns and fears of other groups among the country's population. Strong anxiety and fear of people of their own ethnic group were expressed by 17 percent of Russians living in Lithuania, 8 percent of Poles, and 7 percent of Lithuanians. It is reasonable to assume that the process of de-Russification of Lithuania, which began in the late 1980s and continued after the country gained its independence, may have contributed to how some ethnic Russians felt about their role in Lithuanian society. Psychologically, some ethnic Russians in Lithuania identify themselves as "Russians" and do not want to assimilate and accept a new Lithuanian identity. On the other hand, many Russians are trying to assimilate into Lithuania's mainstream culture. In addition, and this perhaps contributes to a relatively low level of negative ethnic attitudes in the country, Lithuania did not have as pressing a citizenship problem for the

Russian-speaking population as its neighbours, Latvia and Estonia, had in the 1990s. This does not mean that Lithuania cared little about protecting its sovereignty and identity. In 1990, for example, four ethnic Poles attempted to push forward an initiative that would have resulted in the creation of a Polish autonomous region on the territory of Lithuania inhabited mostly by ethnic Poles. These individuals were tried and imprisoned for their activities (PAP, 1999).

Many Lithuanians, but not a clear majority of them, express concerns about non-Lithuanians residing in their country. Approximately every fourth person out of ten surveyed suggested that he or she worries about "prevalence of immigrants who do not want or are not able to assimilate to our culture, language, and style of life." There is a sizeable proportion of undocumented aliens in Lithuania, people who either entered this country illegally or overstayed terms of their visas. It is estimated that most of these undocumented individuals tend to move further to Europe. Although the proportion of immigrants is very low, there are ongoing debates on whether Lithuania is tolerant enough to accept refugees and other immigrants from countries such as Afghanistan, Turkey, Somalia, and others. For instance, nearly 23 percent of Lithuanians expressed some concern about the "invasion of Islam" in their country. In light of these data, it is not a surprise that almost 50 percent of people express at least some concerns about a complete loss of Lithuania's traditions and culture. Despite these concerns, fear of the country's overpopulation is among the last items on the list of the respondent's worries.

Fears of internal enemies and worries about plots against the country are relatively insignificant but they cannot be ignored. There are sizeable groups of people who acknowledge the existence of some "internal" threats. Slightly more than 13 percent of people worry about "KGB activity" (in spite of the fact that this organization does not exist in Lithuania) and people perhaps express their concerns about KGB spying activities directed from some neighbouring countries, including Russia. Suggestions about the Masons and their attempt to "seize the world" worry less than 5 percent of the population. Similarly, the existence of fears about "Jewish conspiracy" was confirmed by as low as 5 percent of the interviewees. It is unusual that this xenophobic idea was supported by more than 9 percent of college-educated public.

Overall, the single-digit number does not allow the analyst to argue about the existence of an anti-Semitic trend in Lithuanian public opinion. A reasonable explanation can be given after a more careful analysis of the sample and the context of the interview. On the other hand, a tendency of highly-educated people to hold negative opinions against particular groups is not Lithuania's unique feature. The same tend was described in other countries, such as the United States (Bolce and DeMaio, 1999).

Foreign Threats

Lithuania is a small and conveniently located country on the seacoast. The country had only few natural obstacles to prevent invasions and intrusions. Throughout the country's long history, numerous foreign enemies threatened its people. Societal catastrophes, such as carnage, destruction, and plunder, left deep scars in the collective memory of Lithuanians. The Mongol invasions and Turks incursions devastated the country from the south and east. At different times Teutonic Knights, Polish, Swedish, and German kings from the west rode their horses and led their armed men through Lithuania's plains. For many years, this country lived under umbrellas of numerous campaigns of *Polonization, Prussification,* or *Russification.* Finally Soviet invasion in 1939, Nazi occupation in 1941, and then, again, the returning of Soviet troops in 1944, marked history of Lithuania in the twentieth century and represented the major points in the lives of at least three generations of Lithuanians. Should Lithuanians be afraid of losing the country's independence again? How deep are their concerns about foreign adversaries?

Overall, concerns about nuclear war were expressed by 75 percent of people, and 31 percent experienced either strong anxiety or constant fear about proliferation of nuclear weapons. However, only less than 7 percent said they have constant fear of a nuclear war, and almost 20 percent said they do not have this fear at all. Fear of Lithuania's incorporation into Russia was not substantial: Only 12 percent of respondents felt this threat. Altogether, 39 percent of people suggested that they have no fear of Russia at all. There is a significant gap between followers of "left-wing" and "right-wing" parties: The left are less concerned about Russia's threat (only 4 percent of them acknowledged the existence of this fear). On the other hand, 24 percent of those who affiliate themselves with the "right-wing" parties expressed their worries about Russian expansionism. As we mentioned earlier in this chapter, some Lithuanians also revealed their worries about the KGB. Specifically, almost every fourth person who supports "right" parties (for instance, the Conservative Party) believes that the KGB threat exists. Only 7 percent of "leftists" said they were concerned about this organization's activities.

In 1993, the last Soviet-era soldier left Lithuania for good. A year later, the president submitted a formal letter to NATO Secretary General requesting Lithuania's membership in this organization. In 2000, Lithuania started the European Union Accession Negotiations. In 1998, Lithuanians elected President Valdas Adamkus—a former American citizen with Lithuanian ethnic background. Throughout the 1990s and beyond, the majorities of Lithuanians expressed positive attitudes about closer ties of their country with the West—in particular, their positive attitudes about the European Union and Lithuania's inclusion in NATO—thus revealing low levels of concerns and fears of the West. According to a public opinion survey conducted by the public opinion research center Vilmorus in April 2000, 65 percent of Lithuanians approved of their country's membership in the European Union, an eight-point increase compared to 1999 surveys (Baltic News Service, April 19, 2000).

Many individuals during the years of transformation were able to learn about the benefits of foreign trade and tourism. The country typically hosts scores of German and Polish holiday-makers, especially during summers, which brings extra cash to many Lithuanians working in the tourist industry or associated with tourism (BNS, 1999). Lithuanians, meanwhile, expressed different opinions about foreigners and close to half of the population revealed their concerns about the extent to which foreign countries and their representatives participate in business with Lithuania. A survey administered by Vilmorus (the study was commissioned by the Lithuanian Foreign Affairs Ministry) revealed that only slightly more than 50 percent of Lithuanians believed that giving foreigners the right to purchase land in Lithuania would have several positive effects. Some 49 percent of respondents said that if they had agricultural land to sell they would give priority to those who offered the best price, regardless of the buyer's ethnic origin or citizenship. However, there was a cautious attitude expressed toward foreigners in Lithuania: More than 42 percent said that in land deals they would give a priority to Lithuanian citizens (Baltic News Service, August 1, 2000).[3]

Other surveys suggest that an opposition to a "foreign economic invasion" exists and people's concerns may be very strong. More than one in six Lithuanians did not approve of the sale of Mazeikye-Nafta petroleum complex to the United States; this deal was persistently labeled as disadvantageous to Lithuania (Burbulis, 1999). Such anti-Western opinions may be easily discounted and treated as completely rational attitudes: People simply want to protect property that, they believe, belongs to them. However, some politicians express their anxious thoughts about these tendencies and call them xenophobic. For instance, Landsbergis, the speaker of the Lithuanian Parliament, conveyed his worry about radical anti-Western attitudes, which started to be disseminated in Lithuania by anti-American and other nationalist forces in the late 1990s. In his view, anti-Western attitudes may develop along with the growing proportion of U.S. investments in the Lithuanian economy and the "invasion" of mass culture from across the ocean. Overall, almost 39 percent of Lithuanians express some concern about the process of "Americanisation" of cultural and social life in Lithuania.

It is important to mention that differences in the views of the people with different ethnic backgrounds were quite significant in each country included in our project. In Lithuania the views of the majorities of ethnic Lithuanians and ethnic Russians were different on almost every political and social issue. For instance, 36 percent of the Russians said in 1998 that they "would be better off if we were still part of the Soviet Union"; only 18 percent of the Lithuanians held the same view (Vilmorus, 1997).

Other Worries

As in most polls conducted in democratic societies, when people are asked an open-ended or a multiple-choice question about the biggest concern or problem they are facing today there is a slim chance that many respondents will produce a similar distribution of answers: Typically, the responses are quite diverse (see appendix to this chapter). One problem may seem the most troubling for a particular individual whereas another chooses a different item on the list. For example, the growing crime rate was named the biggest problem by 18 percent of Lithuanians in a survey in which its respondents had to pick the most worrisome, from their view, problem (Burbulis, 1999). However, when respondents are asked to evaluate every item on a survey, the results can be quite different. For example, when respondents were asked to assess their fear about "criminalization of society" in Lithuania, 46 percent of them reported having anxiety and constant fear. Concerns about crime were among the most salient during the ten years of transition and may be similar to fears and worries expressed by people in other post-Soviet states. People in bigger cities express greater worries about crime than those who live in small towns and villages. Worries about corruption in government were expressed by almost 44 percent of people. According to people's opinions (February, 1999), the most corrupt individuals were police officers, physicians, and lawyers. Constant fear of terrorism was expressed by 5 percent of respondents, and great deal of anxiety about terrorism was mentioned by 26 percent. These results were obtained before the terrorist attacks against the United States.

Before the anthrax scare of 2001, about 53 percent of Lithuanians felt strong anxiety and constant fear about mass epidemics, the spread of AIDS, and "other lethal diseases." Such concerns may be considered as based on rational evaluations of reality: Health problems are not among the least important for Lithuanians. Even though such fears exist, they do not necessarily change people's behavior. As an illustration, let us refer to the results of a World Health Organization's poll conducted in 1995. The poll revealed that people in Lithuania at that time knew enough about AIDS, but their sexual behavior—including behavior that involves practicing safe sex—had not changed as a result of their knowledge (Baltic News Service, October 2, 1995). However, this international survey was taken two years prior to an outburst of AIDS in the neighboring Kaliningrad region, a part of Russia, which could have increased people's awareness about the disease.

Compared to other worries and fears, Lithuanians are less concerned about natural disasters. About 26 percent of the surveyed mentioned persistent anxiety about these potential developments. Other environmental problems are sources of concerns for relatively large groups of Lithuanians. Ozone holes in the atmosphere are sources of worries for 30 percent, who mentioned persistent anxiety. The destruction of forests on the planet concerned 23 percent of the respondents.

In summary, fears about the future are more common in middle-aged generations, people with lower educational levels, and those who live in the province. The pessimism is typical for those who could not adjust to the transforming social reality in the country. Moreover, uncertainty and frustration about the future is likely to be expressed by those people whose candidates lose elections. There is one important trend in people's attitudes that can be important for the evaluation of the received data: Even though individuals indicate the sources of their anxiety and fear, many of them express very low confidence about whether they are able to overcome these obstacles and change the situation.

Altogether slightly more than 50 percent of those who support this passive viewpoint are among low-educated population, lowest income group, retirees, and residents of rural areas. There are significantly less passive-oriented responses among college-educated people and individuals with the highest incomes (29 percent in each group). The same attitudinal pattern is noticeable in the answers to the question "If this disaster takes place what would be your reaction?" The most "active," i.e., action-oriented attitudes, were expressed largely by college-educated, high-income professionals from urban areas.

Table 7.1 Distribution of Answers to the Question: "What Kinds of Problems Disturb You and to What Degree?"

Possible Disasters and Calamities	It Doesn't Concern Me	The Chance of This Disturbs Me			Don't Know
		Some Concern	*Strong Anxiety*	*Constant Fear*	
1. Nuclear war	19.6	42.9	26.2	6.7	4.7
2. Terrorism	17.8	46.1	26.3	5.0	4.8
3. Attack of neighbouring states	31.8	45.5	13.9	2.2	6.7
4. Civil war	35.9	37.6	17.5	3.5	5.5
5. Genocide (i.e., mass repressions of people by their ethnic and national identity)	46.0	30.7	12.9	2.2	8.3
6. Seizure of power by extremists or by mafia	26.6	44.9	18.3	4.4	5.7
7. Dictatorship and mass repressions	37.3	36.6	15.6	2.2	8.4
8. Catastrophic crop failure	31.5	39.2	19.2	2.4	7.8
9. Natural disasters	21.7	45.3	22.4	3.6	6.9
10. The end of this world	46.6	27.4	11.3	4.5	10.1

Table 7.2 Distribution of Answers to the Question: "In this Part We Request You to Mark Down How Much You Are Afraid of the Following Disasters:"

Possible Disasters and Calamities	*It Doesn't Disturb Me*	*The Chance of This Caused Me*			*Don't Know*
		Some Concern	*Strong Alarm*	*Constant Fear*	
23. Mass unemployment	7.1	39.7	43.8	8.9	0.5
24. Criminalization of the society	7.9	43.1	39.8	6.0	3.2
25. Corruption of administrative structures	10.4	43.1	39.1	4.4	2.9
26. Break-up of the family	17.6	53.6	21.5	2.9	4.3
27. Complete lawlessness	6.3	50.9	34.4	5.0	3.3
28. Dangerous overpopulation of cities	59.5	26.5	4.2	0.4	9.4
29. Accumulation of unused waste products	28.0	50.4	13.2	1.3	7.1
30. Decline of the general level of life; impoverishment	5.3	40.9	42.4	9.4	2.0
31. Prevalence of immigrants, who don't want or are not able to assimilate our culture, language, style of life	23.8	45.0	21.8	3.5	5.8
32. Loss of feeling of collectivism, mutual aid, extreme "individualism"	24.3	50.3	13.5	1.9	10.0

Notes

1. One event also attracted the attention of the world media. In 1998, Mr. Adamkus, a 71-year-old Lithuanian American, defeated his much younger Lithuania-born opponent and became the country's new president.
2. According to this survey Lithuanians identify themselves as follows: 84 percent Catholics, 2 percent other confessions, 10 percent non-believers, and 3 percent found it difficult to answer; Latvians: 23 percent Catholics, 38 percent Lutherans, 2 percent Orthodox Church believers, 4 percent other confessions, 31 percent non-believers, and 2 percent difficult to answer; Estonians: 40 percent Lutherans, 7 percent Orthodox Church believers, 5 percent other confessions, 32 percent non-believers, and 17 percent difficult to answer.
3. Up to the recent past, foreign companies were not allowed to buy land but could lease it for up to 99 years (BNS, 1999).

Chapter 8

Russian Immigrants in America: Fears and Hopes

Samuel Kliger

Since the late 1980s, a new wave of Russian immigrants, commonly called "the fourth wave," started to come to the United States. The first wave of Russians was part of the historic nineteenth and early twentieth century immigration to the United States. After World War II, a second wave of immigrants took advantage of the chaotic conditions in Europe to flee to the United States. Starting with a change in immigration law in the early 1970s, a third wave of immigrants from the former Soviet Union came, along with the much more massive tsunami of immigrants from around the world, particularly Latin America and Asia.

The third and, especially, the fourth wave, which started in the late 1980s and early 1990s, have brought almost 400,000 people—mostly refugees—to the United States (Galperin, 1996). More than half of all these refugees settled in New York City. If we add those who came with other types of immigrant visas (such as close relatives of American citizens, asylum seekers, employment-based visa holders and green card lottery winners), the number of Russian immigrants probably has hit 400,000 in the New York metropolitan area alone. New Russian immigrants seem to be reaching a "critical mass" with a high degree of political, cultural and economic agitation, opening the possibility for a sharp rise in institutional and social growth.

For the sake of simplicity, this chapter refers to survey respondents as "Russian immigrants," "immigrants," "Russian-speaking immigrants," and "new Russian immigrants" (NRI). Despite the fact that the entire group includes a variety of ethnic and sub-ethnic groups (like Bukharian Jews, Ukrainians, Georgians), we use these terms to represent Russian-speaking immigrants from the different regions and republics of the former Soviet Union.

Socioeconomic Status, Identity, Satisfaction, and Adaptation

Approximately 57 percent of adult immigrants in New York are less than 55 years old. The time one has lived in America is one of the strongest indicators of immigrants' achievements, economic status, and attitudes. For the sake of simplicity, we call these groups "the freshmen" (less than three years), "the sophomores" (three to less than six years), "the juniors" (six to less than nine years), and "the seniors"—those who live in America for nine years or more.

After just a few years of being in America, immigrants dramatically change most of the components of their status and some of their attitudes. The employment rate jumps from 29 percent within "the freshmen" to 65 percent among "the seniors." For those under 65 years old, 70 percent of "the juniors" and 82 percent of "the seniors" are employed. The number of immigrant families with incomes of $40,000 and above increases from only 2 percent for the "youngest" residents to 30 percent for those more than nine years in America (the American Jewish Committee, 2000). Russian immigrants are the most educated immigrant group in American immigration history. They are even more educated than American Jews as a group (Annual Survey of American Jewish Opinion, 1998). Moreover, their striving for education continues. Approximately 28 percent of all respondents either have received American education or are enrolled in American colleges (not including those who are studying ESL).[1] The average annual income of a Russian immigrant family in New York is only about $15,000. However, among the employed part of immigrant population the average income is $27,500, while the average income of the employed residing in America for more than six years is $34,500. Thus, working and residing in America for more than six years most likely bring a Russian immigrant family into the American middle class.

The Russian-speaking community of New York (and apparently in the United States) is a multicultural enclave: It is simultaneously ethnic (53 percent), immigrant (44 percent), American (25 percent) and cosmopolitan (3 percent). Russian ethnic identity is strongly expressed by about 45 percent of immigrants, though in the majority of cases in combination with other identities ("Russian immigrant," "Russian Jew," "American of Russian origin"). Most of the Russian immigrants, young or old, have become citizens (23 percent) or are planning to become citizens (77 percent). Over two thirds (67 percent) plan on becoming citizens within three years.

In general, cross-cultural studies have revealed that a high life-satisfaction rate is a strong indicator of social stability and vice versa. A Russian immigrant with high life-satisfaction most likely feels integrated into his or her new cultural environment. A large portion (44 percent) of Russian immigrants in New York are either completely or mostly satisfied with their life in America. We can observe that satisfaction rate increases dramatically with time lived in this country. The satisfaction rate (those who said they are completely or mostly satisfied with their life here) grows from 28 percent for the "freshmen" to 64 percent for the "seniors." Even the "freshmen," or those immigrants who live in America for less then three years, express a satisfaction rate two times higher than Russians in Russia (see chapter on Russia).

To the degree that Russian immigrants are dissatisfied with their life, they still feel "Russian" or "immigrant." Conversely, those who say they are "Americans" seldom say that they are dissatisfied with their lives (4 to 5 percent). Those who say they are "just an immigrant" or "Russian" are four times as likely to be dissatisfied with their life (18 to 19 percent). Apparently, the satisfaction with life in America is related to feeling that many immigrants have found a home for their values.

Fears and Immigration

As it was stated earlier in this chapter, Russian immigrants expose at least four categories of fears. First, to the extent the Russian immigrants represent Soviet and post-Soviet society, their fears are similar to those that Russians feel, being trapped between the two worlds: communist and post-communist social realities. In a sense, these are the fears that were essential to "old" Soviet society and were taken without much transformation into the "new" social environment of post-communist Russia. For the sake of simplicity, let us call these fears "inert fears." This set of fears is resistant to most changes in "hard" or "soft" reality. A good example is a fear of "nuclear war." Indeed, it was created during the Cold War era by the real confrontation between the superpowers ("hard reality"). This confrontation has been perceived by Soviet people as a real danger or threat of nuclear war, and has been reinforced by Soviet propaganda and media ("soft reality"). While both realities—hard and soft—have been changed dramatically after the end of the Cold War era, the fear of "nuclear war" is still one of the most "popular" fears shared by 36 to 37 percent of people in both groups—Russians in Russia and Russian immigrants in America.[2]

The same is true for such fears as "natural disaster" and the possibility of "returning to mass repression." Since Russia historically did not suffer much from "natural disasters" such as earthquakes or floods, the likelihood of "natural disaster" was and still is not very high. Nevertheless, a significant minority of people in the Soviet Union and in Russia feel "strong alarm" or "constant fear" about natural disaster. And though the number of people expressing this fear went slightly down for the past ten years, it is still high in post-Soviet Russia as well as among immigrants who just took it from Russia and bear it intact.

The fear of "return to mass repression" has very interesting dynamics. In 1989, when the likelihood of such an event was apparently high (as was later proven by the 1991 coup), Russians seemingly underestimated it, expressing "strong alarm" or "constant fear" at the level of only 14 percent. By 1996, this rate has doubled, leading a sizeable minority (28 percent) to be strongly afraid of mass repression, though any objective analysis demonstrated that return to mass repression in Russia is hardly possible. Even in 1999, while the "real" possibility of mass repression became invisible 21 percent of Russians were still attached to that fear. As for the immigrants, they express this fear in significantly higher level than Russians in Russia (39 percent) illustrating two motives they possibly have. One is based upon a psychological effect that their fear of possible return to mass repression in Russia may reflect their attempt to justify their decision to immigrate. The second is the old, "inert" fear inherited in immigrants' consciousness from all-Soviet fears of totalitarian regime.

We consider the fear of "contamination" to be also one of the "inert" fears that people started to experience in the late-Soviet period and continue to express in post-Soviet Russia as well as in immigration. And again, the higher number of immigrants expressing this fear in comparison with the Russians may be a reflection of their justification for immigration.

Fears Related to New Realities in Russia

This category of fears reflects dramatic changes in Russia in the 1990s (see the chapter on Russia). As a result, we can see dramatic changes in people's feelings of threat and dangers. Except for the personal issues and existential fears, such as sickness of children, physical pain, or fear of death, Soviet people expressed two main and deep concerns: nuclear war and natural disaster. Two other strong anxieties—extinction of humanity and tyranny and lawlessness—were presented at a rate two times lower. And the third category of fears that was expressed by relatively small numbers of 12 to 17 percent of the population in the late-Soviet period were those of poverty, criminals, return to mass repression, and national conflicts.

The picture completely changed in Russia in the 1990s. The fears of criminals, poverty, and lawlessness are expressed on a very high level by 65 to 70 percent of Russians. Fear of crime and criminals—that only 15 percent of people experienced in 1989–1990 in the Soviet Union—has exploded to a 70 percent level. Fear of poverty, once shared by 17 percent, hit 67 percent, and the fear of lawlessness increased dramatically from 23 to 66 percent. Two other fears—return to mass repression and national conflicts—have also increased significantly: national conflicts from 12 percent to 40 percent, and mass repression from 14 percent to 29 percent. Even the fear of returning to mass repression has not only gone, as one could predict for transition to democratic society period, but instead has grown. Only two fears have slightly diminished: the fear of nuclear war (from 48 to 38 percent) and the fear of natural disaster (from 42 to 35 percent).

For most of the fears examined, immigrants follow the pattern of post-Soviet Russians. They fear almost at the same rate as Russians do the new realities of post-communist Russia: tyranny, lawlessness, poverty, criminals, and national conflicts. Fear of mass unemployment is less explainable, while the fear of terrorism is explainable higher among immigrants. In the case of terrorism, the explanation of this "exaggeration" is that immigrants not only feel compassion for Russians but they also are afraid of real terrorism on American soil. In case of mass unemployment, immigrants' fear reflects only compassion to their former compatriots.

The only exception is the fear of the return to communist rule. While Russians are afraid of this event less through the course of time (22 percent in 1996 and only 9 percent in 1999), Russian immigrants feel the threat on a level of almost 40 percent. Such an exaggerated fear of communists among immigrants may be attributed to their willingness to justify their decision to immigrate.

An excellent illustration of how Russian immigrants in America are close to Russians in Russia is their attitudes toward the 1999 conflict in Yugoslavia. Our survey had a remarkable opportunity to gauge how immigrants wrestle with new identities and the disruptions of having a new homeland when the conflict heated up. A significant majority of Russian immigrants were opposed to the NATO air strikes against Yugoslavia. The profile of their opinions was almost an exact reverse of the opinions of the general population of Americans, and similar to the opinions of Russians in Russia: Almost 59 percent of Russian immigrants opposed the air strikes (the American Jewish Committee, 2000, p. 54.)[3] Two thirds of Russian immigrants don't think the U.S./NATO air strikes will seriously damage U.S.-Russian relations. They seem to find the Yugoslavia conflict a very uncomfortable nuisance to U.S.-Russian feelings but subsidiary to the countries' long-term relations. It appears that immigrants believe that Russia is willing to let the United States/NATO have its way with Yugoslavia at the expense of only some bruised feelings. Even opponents of the air campaign do not think that U.S.-Russian relations will be harmed.

Specific Immigrants' Fears

While immigrants immerse themselves in new social contexts in America and obtain new concerns and fears corresponding to their new environment, they are (especially those who are new to America) still attached to their old homeland. Paradoxically, they fear more about Russia's future than they do about the future of their generation, their ethnic group, their city, the future of people of the same social strata, the future of our planet, and even the future of America.

Among the most intense specific fears that immigrants have are fears of hostile forces, such as genocide or persecution of people based on their origin or religion, and the spread of neo-Nazism and similar forces. Under these categories, many are afraid of anti-Semitism in Russia. Forty-eight percent of Russian immigrants expressed "constant fear" or "strong anxiety" about genocide or persecution of people in Russia according to their ethnicity or nationality. In contrast, only 16 percent of Russians expressed the same opinion. Similarly, just 18 percent of Russians expressed their strong concerns about the spread of neo-Nazism, whereas this attitude was expressed by 56 percent of immigrants.

An endless debate about anti-Semitism in Russia and in the republics of the former Soviet Union has been extended and intensified during last few years after the collapse of the former Soviet Union. In contemporary studies of anti-Semitism in Russia there are two different sets of facts and data. One suggests that anti-Semitism in Russia is no longer a threat or danger for Jews there, and that the level of anti-Semitism in Russia is comparable to the level of anti-Semitism in the United States and other developed countries. The other implies that Anti-Semitism is a real danger (Gudkov and Levinson, 1994).

Whatever the actual state of anti-Semitism in Russia is, Russian immigrants are very sensitive toward this issue. The Research Institute for New Americans in a study sponsored by the American Jewish Committee (1999–2000, p. 30) has found that Russian immigrants in New York are very emphatic that anti-Semitism is a serious problem in the former Soviet Union. This opinion is in striking contrast to those who say anti-Semitism in Russia is low. Eighty-five percent of 1,024 respondents said that they believe anti-Semitism in the Former Soviet Union is a "very serious" or "serious" problem, while only 34 percent feel that anti-Semitism is a "very serious" or "serious" problem in America.

Whereas the previous wave of immigrants of the 1970s and the 1980s was oppressed by the Soviet system that seemed to offer no friendly future for Jews, the current wave of the 1990s is leaving Russia because they are afraid that the Russian government will not persist into the future. The previous wave saw their future blocked because of their Jewishness. The fourth wave sees some advancements for Jews in Russia but disbelieve its stability.

Further, today if Russian Jews have a strong Jewish religious identity they migrate to Israel. Those who now come to the United States are not coming so much for Jewish reasons but for fear of Russia's collapse. Consequently, the current wave is less orientated to discovering its Jewish identity in the United States. It is to Russia that their hopes and fears have been most attuned to, though the undercurrent of Russian anti-Semitism has kept Jewish identity alive.

Immigrants, of course, have very diverse fears. On the whole, however, while sharing with Russians similar structure of fears, Russian immigrants in America have a similar profile of anxieties to Russians (see table 8.1.)

While exposing a high level of social anxiety, both Russian immigrants in America and Russians in Russia have quite different views on their future. Immigrants are more assured about their future in America (51 percent of them in 1999) than Russians are about their future in Russia (20 percent in 1999). Among immigrants, 33 percent were either uncertain or mostly uncertain about their future. In contrast, 68 percent of Russians expressed the same attitudes about their future. Fifty-five percent of Russian immigrants assert that their life in America is more secured than it was in Russia, while only 8 percent said it is less secured.

While a significant majority of the immigrants (70 percent) stand up for market economy and for integrating Russia into world community, they

Table 8.1 Anxiety from a Comparative Perspective. Percent of Those Who Agreed with the Following Statements.

	Russians in Russia (1996)	*Russians in Russia (1999)*	*Immigrants (1999)*
Relations with other people have become very difficult	32	32	23
Your dreams are interrupted by nightmares	28	29	27
You become nervous and irritated	49	43	44
Thoughts about your job pursue you every day	32	31	48
You have lost control over making any decisions	12	9	13
You find it difficult to deal with hardships	34	34	37
You are object of critique and hostility	18	16	19
Everything around you has become strange and odd	16	16	14

are almost three times less likely to support the idea of reconstruction of Russia as a great power, so they are in a sense less "patriotic." In answering the question "What political regime is desirable for modern Russia?," 37 percent of Russians and 46 percent of immigrants said "president republic." Twenty-two percent of Russians and 23 percent of immigrants voted for "parliament republic." Votes for Soviet regime are 35 percent of Russians and about 3 percent of the immigrants. About half of both Russians (45 percent) and Russian immigrants (51 percent) support "mixed economy," e.g., a combination of state and private property, market and plan. Yet, in 1999, only 8 percent of Russians and 29 percent of immigrants were for strengthening of private property and development of market reforms. Twenty-five percent of Russians support state property and planned economy, while only 5 percent percent of immigrants do so.

The strongest motive for leaving Russia for both immigration groups is "interests of other family members and reunification of the family." More than 75 percent of immigrants have mentioned this reason as a motive of leaving Russia. For many, especially elderly people, immigration is a tragedy and a constant fear. Nineteen percent of them said they feel "strong nostalgia" and 33 percent just feel nostalgic.

Conclusion

The interpretation of the data survey of Russian immigrants is based on several assumptions. First, recent immigrants from the former Soviet Union are—in many essential aspects—products of the Soviet system and therefore bear similar structure of basic fears as Soviet people in general. In a sense, Russian immigrants represent a splinter of the late Soviet Union and, in some aspects, current Russian society. Second, the immigrants reflect specific frustrations: They are challenged by their new immigrant status, they encounter new and often hard realities of living in America (cultural shock, language barriers, loss of social status, etc.), they continue to be attached psychologically to their former homeland (Russia, Ukraine, etc). Many of them are Jewish and therefore they may have some specific fears related to their past experience (and, specifically, discrimination against them) and fears about future of their friends and relatives in the former Soviet Union. Next, the fears of new Russian immigrants expose a mixture of recollections of "old" fears people experienced back in Russia, reflections of "old" fears (that is a perception of fears they think they would feel had they still stayed in Russia), and "new" fears created by a new social environment. Finally, fears immigrants demonstrate in their new homeland regarding their old homeland are mostly created by "soft reality" rather than "hard reality." "Hard reality" is a reflection of real objective danger in society, while "soft reality" is a mental construction, which can be influenced by ideology, culture, mass media, and historic memories.

Notes

1. Twenty percent of those participants in American education (or about 6 percent of total) completed graduate study in America, 16 percent (or about 5 percent of all immigrants) graduated from an American college. An additional 17 percent of the total are studying English now. Another 12 percent of the sample attended college, and about 5 percent attended graduate school. Six percent attend computer courses and 4 percent professional training programs.
2. Data are taken from all-Russia survey by the Russian Academy of Sciences (July 1996). The figures indicate only those who expressed "strong anxiety" or "constant fear." In all-Union survey by VTSIOM respondents choose from a list of fears in answering the question "What are you most afraid of?" Sources: *New Outlook: A quarterly publication of the American Committee on U.S.-Soviet Relations,* vol. 1, no 3, summer 1990, p. 32. See also: Samuel Kliger and Paul de Vries, 1993, "The Ten Commandments in Soviet People's Consciousness" in S.P. Ramet (ed.), *Religious Policy in the Soviet Union,* Cambridge University Press, N.Y. 1993, p. 191. "Catastrophic Mood in Contemporary World." Questionnaire, Linear Distribution." Moscow. 1996. See also: Vladimir Shubkin. Strakhi v Rossii (Fears in Russia). Sotsiologicheskii Zhurnal, 1997, no. 3, p. 69; Vladimir Shubkin. *Katastroficheskoye Soznaniye v Sovremennom Mire* (Catastrophic Consciousness in Contemporary World), 1999, a data, manuscript, p. 3.
3. It seems that attitudes toward the Kosovo conflict were formed mostly by media ("soft reality"). The feelings about the air strikes were quite intense. Most Russian media in Russia and in New York featured bold headlines and editorial attacks against the NATO air strikes. The media coverage greatly affected people in Russia and, maybe, immigrants as well. An extraordinarily large number of the respondents felt the necessity to qualify or explain their answers. Consequently, we may infer that the opinions aren't solidified. The emotional reaction to the air strikes is high but diffuse. Even among those opposed to the air strikes one third don't offer an alternative to what the United States/NATO is doing.

Chapter 9

A Conclusion: Transitional Fears in the Post-Communist World

Eric Shiraev and Vladimir Shlapentokh

In the fall of 2001, anti-terrorist fever reached Eastern Europe. Police patrols and armored vehicles on the streets, anti-aircraft batteries near nuclear power plants, tough security procedures at airports, concrete walls around U.S. diplomatic and military facilities—all these and other extraordinary measures reflected the overall state of anxiety. In the 1990s, the ex-communist countries made huge steps toward the integration with the West. As a result, many people in these countries had to face an inevitable development: their countries were perceived to be under the same threat as the United States' key allies following the terror attacks of 2001. In various polls conducted in October of that year, almost 50 percent of these countries' population expressed concerns about a treat of a new global war (Szamado, 2001). For many, their future seemed not as certain as it was yesterday.

Overall State of Mood

Psychological research shows that a person's lack of confidence in the future may be linked to this individual's fears and concerns: If the future is uncertain, it enhances fear of it, which is generally called anxiety. Likewise, anxiety increases the feeling of uncertainty. What do survey data suggest about people's attitudes about their future during such an unprecedented societal transformation?

Before the dramatic events of the late 1980s, people of the East European communist countries, even though they had to accommodate their life to the conditions of totalitarian society, tended to look at the future without great fears. Anyone who was not openly against the regime was certain that his or her job, education, access to medical service, pensions, and living accommodations were guaranteed by the government. Economies were stable, unemployment did not exist, violent crime and social order were generally under control. People had no significant fears of political instability. Social anxiety in communist countries was mostly fueled by the threat of ecological dangers and, to some degree, by the danger of nuclear war. However, the intensity of these fears was quite low.

Official ideology in communist countries was an important source of popular optimism. Being an excellent example of social demagoguery, communist ideology appealed to important and attractive ideas such as national patriotism, social equality, and humanitarian values. Many individuals believed in their countries' moral and cultural superiority over the West and advantages of the planning system of economy over free-market capitalism. Government was seen not only as a powerful institution of coercion but also as the major provider of social security and other benefits. In addition, focusing on an optimistic vision of the future, the government was able to maintain a certain level of optimism among many people in countries of the communist bloc (see, for example, Orlova, 1983). For example, the Soviet leadership was very much concerned about the development in Soviet people of positive, hopeful, and upbeat attitudes about future: The official ideology successfully banned any attempt to introduce any elements of pessimism, gloom, or doubt in publications about the future of the country.

The core idea of societal stability, greatness of socialist society, was generally accepted by the masses. Even though liberal intellectuals and dissidents of the former communist countries were hoping to see the end of the oppressive regimes, the vast majority of them could not predict that the system would collapse so rapidly and with so little resistance from governments (Shlapentokh, 1990).

The political and social situation in the communist countries changed immensely in the late 1980s and early 1990s. At the initial stages of the transition process, most people in these countries remained confident in the radical improvement of their life under the umbrella of liberal reforms. According to VTSIOM data, about one quarter of the Russians met the new year of 1991 with hope and only 9 percent with fears (VTSIOM archive, no. 108, section 17). After 1991, the number of people who were optimistic never reached this rather high level of the earlier days of the transition. A slight majority of all East Europeans said there was more respect than nonrespect for human rights in their countries. However, in the former republics of Soviet Union and the Baltic states, the majority took a more negative view (*The Guardian,* 1993).

Despite difficulties and setbacks, most people expressed little desire to restore communism back in their countries. Although about half the Russian people in 1996 stated that things were better in the past (*The Economist,* 1996), the specific idea about the restoration of communism was not shared by majorities of people in other countries. In Poland, for instance, where an ex-communist was elected president, only 8 percent wanted a communist economic and political system back. In Hungary, there were 20 percent of those who felt nostalgic for communism. This idea was supported by 29 percent in Bulgaria (New Democracies Barometer, 1996).

In the early 1990s, only one third of East Europeans were on the whole happy about their societies' painful social and political transition. By 1996, the situation has changed. Nearly two thirds of people in Eastern European countries, such as the Czech Republic and Poland (excluding the ex-Soviet countries abutting Russia), were broadly happy about their countries' new political and social system (*New Democracies Barometer,* 1996).

A different pattern of opinion dynamics appeared in Russia. The level of pessimism in Russia increased dramatically after 1992. By 1994, the polling firm VTsIOM found that the number of those who expressed optimism declined to 16 percent and the number of those who had fears about the future increased to 22 percent; in 1998, the respective numbers were at the same level: 12 percent and 24 percent respectively (VTsIOM archive, no. 62, section 1, 1995; no 4, section 15, 1998). When asked at the end of 1994, "Are hard times behind us or in the future?," 9 percent of 3000 respondents of a VTsIOM survey said "in the past" and 52 percent said "in the future." In opinion polls taken in 1994 and 1995, no less than 50 to 60 percent of Russians characterized their mood as tense (VTsIOM, no. 5, 1994; no. 6, 1994; no. 2, 1995, pp. 53, 57). Among them, 11 percent "felt fear of the future" and 40 to 50 percent also regarded the present situation as fraught with "crisis and blast." No less than two thirds of all Russians described the situation in 1992–1994 in their country as gloomy, with no brighter outlook possible for the future. In a VTsIOM survey conducted in August 1994, Russians described the situation in the country as "critical" (40 percent), "alarming" (27 percent), or "catastrophic" (22 percent). Only 6 percent treated the situation as "normal" (*Nezavisimaia Gazeta,* August 17, 1994). Twenty-five percent thought that "the country will continue to slide into the abyss," and 12 percent expected "anarchy" (*Moskovskie Novosti,* January 15, 1995).

Overall, by the middle of the 1990s, most of the population of the post-communist countries said they lived in a situation of uncertainty about their future. One question in the original survey asked respondents: "How sure are you in the future?" The alternatives for an answer were: "Confident," "Rather confident," "Rather unconfident," and "Completely unconfident."

In this case, the percentages above reflected the number of people who used the third and fourth alternatives. As a result, 67 percent of Russians, 65 percent of Ukrainians, 56 percent of Bulgarians, and 53 percent of Lithuanians chose the "unconfident" responses. Less than 10 percent of the population in all surveyed post-communist countries were confident in their future. A decrease in confidence in the mid-1990s was obvious even in a relatively successfully developing country, such as Czech Republic.

Ideological Pluralism and Uncertainty

The ideological disarray in the studied countries contributed to the states of uncertainty and pessimism of the population. Each post-communist society was ideologically polarized, however, to a different extent. In Russia and Ukraine, the polarization was the most significant and no particular ideology in the 1990s could claim overwhelming support in society. In Lithuania and Czech Republic, polarization was not particularly significant.

For example, 32 percent of Russians and 28 percent of Ukrainians supported parties that "stood up for the ideas of socialism"; 31 and 34 percent respectively supported parties that "stood up for the course of market reforms and joining Russia to the world community"; the rest of the population in these countries "did not have any political preferences" (Levada, 1999). The polarization of views in Bulgaria was also quite high, though less than in both Ukraine and Russia: 21 percent voted for "state property and a planned economy"; 25 percent wanted "private property and market economic reforms"; 43 percent of Bulgarians wanted a mixed economy.

People in the studied countries were also split on which political system they preferred. Russians, for instance, were divided almost equally among the supporters of the "presidential republic" (37 percent), the "parliamentary republic" (23 percent), and the "Soviet regime" (34 percent); a significant number of people voted for "monarchy" (7 percent). The differentiation was also quite high on this issue in Ukraine (the numbers were 17, 10, 21 and 2 percent respectively), and in Bulgaria (20, 41, 14 and 12 percent).

The ideological and political battles between the political forces with mutually exclusive values became a serious source of tension and fear of political instability. The lack of a strong official ideology in post-communist Russia, for instance, was evidently one of the major causes of the spread of pessimism in the country and Russian disbelief in "the radiant future."

Is the Basis of Fears Rational?

There have been hot debates about the origin of most fears in society, in particular in post-communist countries. While some authors insist that human fears are mostly rational and reflect the way people perceive real dangers to their life, property, and well being, other authors suggest that most of these fears are irrational, have no basis in reality, and are generally provoked by political forces that could gain political points by scaring people (Abramson and Inglehart, 1995; Crossette, 1999). It is argued that the media—in their hunt for higher ratings—may deliberately spark fear and anxiety in populations. The same goal may be pursued by certain opinion leaders who attempt to boost their popularity ratings by spreading fears (Kostikov, 1999; Glassner, 1999).

In the individual's mind, different types of information that can be used for predictions and particularly information about possible dangers and disasters have different levels of probability from being "hard reality" (based on real events or witness accounts) to being based on speculations or falsities (Goode and Ben-Yehuda, 1994). As our analysis shows, most of the expressed fears in the studied countries tended to be realistic. Conflicts, wars, and other calamities and disasters, after they take place, may considerably enhance people's fears about these events happening again in the future. Holocaust victims, witnesses of earthquakes and tornadoes in California, Turkey, and Armenia all have reasonable arguments to express worries about these calamities in the future. The dissemination of nuclear weapons in the world, the nuclear accident in Chernobyl, and the expansion of world terrorism can also be referred as legitimate events that may cause "rational fears." At the same time, the single occurrence of a tragic event certainly does not account for the total probability of recurrence. People's perception of the future, of course, is shaped by a great variety of conditions.

Economic Fears

In each and every national case examined in the book, people's anxiety about their economic situation was among the most salient concerns and worries. Among several features related to socioeconomic condition, two major elements of economic calamities—impoverishment and mass unemployment—were examined. Capitalism added two important words to people's everyday vocabulary: unemployment and inflation. Although in most studied cases, official joblessness rates did not reach high levels, the threat of unemployment did exist in people's perception. One of the reasons for triggering people's concerns was the fact that for the first time in a nearly 40-year period of history governments no longer guaranteed work to each and every adult citizen.

However, among most serious sources of concerns were very low wages and extremely high prices: the two main determining factors of poverty.

Overall, fear of poverty was expressed to a greater extent than fear of unemployment in all studied countries. The negative impact of both high prices and low wages is that they limit access to resources to millions of people. In all studied countries, the GNP at the time of the surveys was lower than it was in the 1980s and personal income fell down from 30 to 70 percent (*Goskomstat,* 1997; *Statisticheskoie Obozrenie,* 1997).

A series of liberal economic reforms took place in most of the studied nations. In some of them, such as Russia, for example, the pace of the reform was very high. In others, such as Ukraine and Belarus, the reforms were dragging slowly throughout the 1990s and later. However, regardless of how expeditiously national governments tried to push the reforms forward, for large groups of population in all post-communist countries the economic reforms brought a drastic decline in the standards of living. In most of these countries the death rate increased and the birth rate declined. In 1980, in Russia, Ukraine and Bulgaria the death rate was 11 per 1,000; in Lithuania, it was 10 per 1,000. Two decades later, the death rate grew to 15 per 1,000 in Ukraine, 14 in Russia and Bulgaria, and 12 in Lithuania. The birth rate fell from 15 per 1,000 in Ukraine and Bulgaria and 16 in Lithuania and Russia to 9 in Ukraine, Bulgaria, and Russia; the Lithuanian birth rate remained the same (The World Bank, 1999; IBRD, 1999).

Most people in the former Soviet Union believed in 1993 that the creation of a free market economy is a "bad" thing for the country (*The Guardian,* 1993). Even in countries that were doing better economically than others—such as the Czech Republic—more than 70 percent of its population in 1999 worried about inflation and possible unemployment. In 2000, as it is mentioned in the Polish case, more than one half of the Polish population believed that living conditions in their country would worsen in the forthcoming three years.

Fear of Social Instability

Political transitions in post-communist countries did not "produce" much desired and sustained societal stability. Various cabinets were changing under the changing conditions of social and economic situation. In many countries, once popular political leaders—initiators of democratic reforms, such as Lansbergis in Lithuania and Walesa in Poland—were voted out their high offices by popular will. Others, like Havel and Yeltsin, saw their prestige and popularity rating going down. Democracy brought the sense of uncertainty and insecurity in many people's lives. Even though practically none of the studied countries—with Belarus as a possible exception—fell under the rule of authoritarianism and democracy was sustained, most democratic institutions were in the initial stages of their development.

The behavior of the elite in post-communist countries also contributed greatly to social erosion and the resulting feelings of insecurity. Unfortunately, many individuals within the political and economic leadership ring regarded their positions in power mostly as a source of personal gains. Absorbed by short-term interests and using their positions in power to take immediate advantages and personal enrichment, these politicians and officials contributed to the growing sense of people's cynicism about democratic process and their disillusionment in government. Many politicians and officials were continuously locked in a vicious struggle for perks, resources, and political influence. The political immaturity of the elite often resulted in the total disregard for the penury of the masses and democratic procedures.

Many institutions of the government bureaucracy and, particularly, law enforcement agencies were affected by fraud and corruption. International research centers such as Transparency International (1998) ranked Russia (placed 76th out of 85 ranks), Ukraine (69th) and Bulgaria (66th) among the most corrupt countries in the world (the rank 1 was the position of the least corrupt government, whereas the rank 85 was the indicator of most corrupt). The evaluation of this international organization coincided with people's views in these countries. For instance, 77 percent of the Russians, according to a survey by the Public Opinion Foundation in November 1997, believed that corruption was a problem that would remain in the country for many years to come.

Despite growing disillusionment, most people did not want the restoration of authoritarian regimes in their countries. Only 6 percent of East Europeans said in 1996 that they want their government run by generals (*New Democracies Barometer,* 1996). What many individuals were afraid of was a possibility of political destabilization and chaos. This book's data suggest that, in general, the less stable the situation was in the country the greater concerns about instability were expressed. For example, in the mid-1990s, two thirds of Russians and Ukrainians expressed their worries about the threat of social chaos in their countries. This fear was expressed by almost one half of Bulgarians and two fifth of Lithuanians.

It is noticeable that fears of social chaos were more intense in the regions heavily dominated by political opposition to the incumbent government. For instance, for people in the Russian south and southwest—the regions that consistently supported communists in the local and national elections—fears of "complete lawlessness" were expressed by 71 of population, which was somewhat higher that the national rate of 65 percent. Likewise, worries about the "corruption of administrative structures were expressed by 65 percent of Russian "southerners," compared to 53 percent from the national sample. There is not clear explanation, however, whether these particular fears caused more people to support the communist party and its candidates, or whether the communists' effort to persuade their supporters that Russia was "corrupt" and "lawless" were successful.

In the Russian case, a significant proportion of people did not express fears of dictatorship and an authoritarian ruler. As it was mentioned earlier, many people could have expressed little or no concern about an "iron fist" because they genuinely believed that dictatorship or any other form of a "strong" government was the only way to restore and guarantee social order in the entire country and for the entire people.

Compared to the 1980s, the state of public order in post-communist societies worsened in the 1990s. Street crime, extortion, fraud, murder, prostitution and other forms of crime existed prior to the beginning of the democratic transformation. However, under the new political conditions, they flourished. This definitely furthered the process of social erosion in all post-communist countries.

Offenders not only committed crimes against individuals and their property, they penetrated the major branches of the economy as well as the political establishment, entering politics at both the regional and national levels. For instance, Russian officials from the Ministry of Internal Affairs publicly stated that there were members of criminal structures in the local and federal legislatures (Oreshkin, 1998). The shadow economy was an ever-present force in all East European countries. The prevalence of crime and corruption in society blurred the borders between legal and illegal activity, established violence as the only solution to everyday conflicts, and intimidated the public. As a result, many people experienced well-founded fears of violence and crime.

Environmental Worries

According to information policies established by communist governments, reports about serious environmental problems in these countries were typically banned from publication or broadcasting or seriously censored. Although basic information about natural and manmade disasters was often available, the reported facts were incomplete, inaccurate, and often false. Citizens of the communist countries seldom had a chance to learn about many details related to earthquakes, floods, and other disasters and problems that were taking place at that time. Information about air and water pollution was not available to the general public for the same ideological reasons: According to the official doctrine, socialist enterprises were not "supposed to" pollute the environment.

Nevertheless, many people were concerned about ecological problems, and their awareness grew in the 1980s. At this time in many communist countries, popular environmentalist movements started to grow in nations' capitals and big cities. First "overlooked" by authorities, these organizations were responsible for spreading information in which they were sharing their concerns about many real and potential environmental problems that the countries faced. These concerns were well-founded. The overall environmental situation in the communist countries began to deteriorate in the 1960s and 1970s due to substantial industrial growth, the lack of regulations regarding environmental protection, and the official cover-up (Latsis, 1995). Free media in the early 1990s confirmed what many people already knew: There were more environmental problems than previous governments wanted to acknowledge.

The 1986 Chernobyl nuclear accident was perhaps the first major disaster that took place in a communist country that was not covered up by a heavy screen of secrecy. Perhaps there is no country in Eastern Europe, including Ukraine, Belarus, and Russia, of which the population did not suffer from the consequences of the nuclear accident in Chernobyl in 1986 and later. As expected, fear of new nuclear disasters was greater in the countries that were affected from the consequences of the Chernobyl disaster the most: Ukraine and Belarus. However, even in the countries that were not influenced by the explosion directly, the level of fear about nuclear accidents was relatively high. Nuclear power plants were built in these countries (for example, in Ignalina, Lithuania and Sosnovy Bor, Russia) and many people experience reasonable concerns about their own safety in those places too.

Most of environmental fears expressed in surveys were related to people's concerns about local problems. However, about one quarter of the population in the studied countries expressed serious worries about global developments that could have serious environmental consequences for the whole planet. Among these worries were issues such as the destruction of forests and the expansion of ozone holes in the atmosphere. At the time of the surveys, people were apparently less concerned about the accumulation of unused waste products and global warming, which became one major theme of debates in the United States.

Foreign Threats

The break-up of the socialist bloc put an end to the unconditional dominance of the Soviet Union over smaller countries. Despite the fact that it was the Soviet Union's government that kept East European and Baltic countries in line with its policies, it was Russia and Russians who were generally disliked by many people in the former satellite republics and countries. People in Eastern Europe based their negative attitudes—among other issues—on their countries' historical experiences and the legacy of Soviet and Russian political dominance. It is not a surprise that a sizable proportion of population in these countries feared a possibility of the Russian military and political comeback. Their fears were justified in many ways, especially in the face of geopolitical and populist demagoguery of several Russian prominent politicians of the 1990s. Moreover, the proposed unification between Belarus and Russia was a clear demonstration to some people that the "Russian threat" was real.

On the other hand, people of particular social and age groups in East European and Baltic countries expressed their suspicions and worries about Western influence and expansion. A westward growth of NATO and the inclusion of Poland, Hungary, and the Czech republic have triggered these fears, which were also founded on old political and ideology-driven beliefs about the Western threat, fears of cultural expansionism of Germany (in the Czech Republic particularly) and the United States, and general antipathy toward free-market capitalism.

The conflict in Kosovo in 1999 deeply divided the population of the former Eastern bloc. Whereas most East Europeans treated the NATO military campaign as a necessary measure to restore peace in the region, most Russians and Belarusians saw the war in Kosovo as a threat to the region's stability and the United States as a major threat to international peace. With the Balkan crisis unfolding, most Ukrainians shared with Russians their hostile attitude toward NATO. In April 1999, according to the Fund of Public Opinion, 72 percent of the Russians described themselves as "hostile toward the USA." Eighty-one percent of the Ukrainians were also strongly against the NATO's intervention in Kosovo (Kiev International Institute of Sociology, personal communication, October 25, 1999).

During the 1990s, even though Russia lost its economic and military strength, the country's government, opinion leaders, inspired by mass opinion continued their claims for the world leadership (Shiraev and Zubok, 2000). The concept of foreign threats was virtually abandoned in the early 1990s, only to be "restored" again. A range of internal developments stimulated fears of foreign threats among millions of Russians, and opinion polls show this trend. On the other hand, the majority of people in Poland, Lithuania, Czech Republic, and Bulgaria were quite satisfied with their countries' international status and did not feel any serious foreign dangers, although Lithuanians were somewhat more concerned about their neighbors in the east than Bulgarians and Polls. It was noticeable that 54 percent of Bulgarians identified themselves with Europe and only 23 percent with Russia. The fear of "Americanization" was shared by 27 percent of Russians and 18 percent of Ukrainians. This fear was mentioned only by 12 percent of Bulgarians and 8 percent of Lithuanians.

By 1999, the number of Ukrainians who worried about possible foreign attacks was 30 percent; among Russians this number was 21 percent; 16 percent of Lithuanians and 12 percent of Bulgarians expressed such a worry. Similarly, less than one third of Bulgarians and Lithuanians worried about nuclear attacks against them, whereas 41 percent of Russians and 53 percent of Ukrainians did.

Geographical location and events of the past may influence the expression of particular fears. Almost a quarter of the Bulgarians were seriously afraid of "the invasion of Islam," while the same fear in Lithuania and Russia was shared by only 6 percent of the population (in Ukraine, 12 percent). In the list of "bad times" in the past, Bulgarians ranked "the Turkish yoke" in third place (13 percent in the open question); naturally, this period was not on the list of other nations. The same fears had different intensities in Crimea as compared with other Ukrainian regions. Here, the Tartars demanded the restoration of their political rights and went into conflict with the Ukrainian authorities and the Slav population. While almost 20 percent of the people in Crimea had serious misgivings about "the Islam invasion," only 8 percent of the residents of West Ukraine harbored the same anxieties.

Overall, people had enough information conveyed through partisan media and other sources to "legitimize" their fears of foreign countries.

Ethnic Conflicts

The events of the 1990s unfortunately did not and could not resolve old or emerging new ethnic conflicts in the studied countries. Problems and conflicts between Russians and non-Russians were common in Russia itself, as well as in Baltic states and Ukraine. The fear of "civil and ethnic wars" was higher in ethnically diverse societies such as Ukraine (52 percent of people expressed this fear) and Russia (46 percent in 1996 and 29 percent in 1999). In Bulgaria and Lithuania, fear of ethnic war was mentioned by 18 and 21 percent respectively.

New conflicts grew between ethnic majorities and minorities in all countries of the examined sample. Therefore, fears of immigrants' takeover, ethnic backlashes, and terrorism emerged in the early 1990s and continued through the entire decade. Traditionally, minorities experience greater fear of violence against them than do the dominant groups. To illustrate, in Bulgaria slightly more than one half of the surveyed large ethnic groups, such as ethnic Bulgarians and Muslims, expressed fear of a potential ethnic conflict in their country. Among Bulgarian Gypsies, however, 64 percent expressed their worry about ethnic backlash. Expectedly, people in the areas of conflict or adjacent to these areas tend to express greater fears of violence than people in other regions. For example, Russians from southern regions close to the war zone in Chechnya expressed more anxiety about ethnic conflicts than the rest of the country. As an illustration, in 1996, between 41 and 47 percent of Russians in Moscow, St. Petersburg, and other northern and central regions expressed their fear of civil and ethnic conflicts. Among "southerners" the number was higher: 61 percent. Maybe such fears and other ethnic attitudes were related. For instance, fear of "Zionist Jewish conspirators" was mentioned by "southerners" almost twice as many times as it was by people in Russia (11 percent against 6 percent). However, in absolute numbers, the number of people who expressed this fear was quite insignificant. Perhaps it is understandable why Muscovites, who suffered two malicious terrorist attacks in September 1999—after which two apartment complexes were blasted out—were much more fearful of new attacks than those who did not experience this threat. According to a VTSIOM survey in September 1999, 94 percent of Muscovites feared terrorist attacks in the city of Moscow, the amount significantly higher than in other countries and regions (Izgarshev and Zaks, 1999).

Contextual Factors

Fears brought about or enhanced by a tragic event create powerful waves of new fears, which gradually decline unless they are reinforced by similar tragic events. Unfortunately, the period from the late 1980s and through the post-communist transition of the 1990s was filled with many developments that had a significant impact on most people's anxiety. In Russia, violent confrontations during the constitutional crisis of 1993 produced fears of national disintegration and possible chaos. As we mentioned earlier, explosions in Moscow and some other cities in 1999 caused people to express their great concerns about terrorist attacks. NATO's eastward enlargement caused some fear in anti-Western-minded individuals in Poland and the Czech republic and greater fear among large groups of people in their eastern neighbors, such as Belarus, Russia, and Ukraine. The financial crisis of 1998 caused increased fears of economic instability and unemployment in practically all examined countries.

Different Intensities of Fears: "Big" and "Small" Countries

A comparative analysis of a sample consisting of two "big" countries, such as Russia and Ukraine, and two "small" countries, such as Bulgaria and

Lithuania, showed that although the hierarchy of fears (the assigned significance) was more or less similar along the sample, the relative number of people who were exposed to different types of fears and subjective intensity of fears oscillated significantly among countries. In the big countries the intensity was much higher than in small countries in all cases. (See table 9.1.)

On average, the intensity of fear in "big" countries was significantly higher than in "small" ones. People of Ukraine and Russia endured higher levels of fear with respect to possible disasters triggered by various political developments both inside and outside the country. They also worried significantly more than the residents of Lithuania and Bulgaria about their countries' environment and the dangers of technological accidents. Lithuanians, overall, expressed less fear that respondents from Bulgaria, Ukraine, and Russia. Being mostly concerned, according to their responses, about the dangers of a nuclear war and the ethnic Russians in their country, Lithuanians appeared to be completely rational in their perceptions of threats to their society. Overall, economically and politically, Lithuania sustained a more stable pace of development than most countries of post-communist Europe. The differences between the countries included in our project provided us with other evidences in favor of the rationality of fear in the post Communist world.

Fear of political instability was higher in the "big" countries than in the "small." Only the fear of "dictatorship and mass repression" in Russia (19 percent) was almost as low as in Bulgaria (16 percent) and Lithuania (18 percent). The difference was particularly high with respect to the dangers of extremists coming to power in the country. While in Ukraine and Russia about one half of the population (52 and 42 percent) was exposed to this fear, in Bulgaria and Lithuania the number of people with this fear was

Table 9.1 Intensity of Fears in Lithuania, Bulgaria, Russia, and Ukraine

Fears	*"Big" Countries (Russia and Ukraine)*	*"Small" Countries (Bulgaria and Lithuania)*	*Ratio*
Economic disasters	74	52	1.42
Crime	66	49	1.34
Ecological disasters	47	29	1.62
International disasters	38	24	1.58
Political disturbances	32	20	1.60
Loss of "culture"	26	20	1.30
Average percentage	47	32	1.47

only about one quarter of the population (25 and 23 percent). Terrorism also produced more fear in the Russia and Ukraine than in the Lithuania and Bulgaria (54 percent in Ukraine and 37 in Russia, against 29 in Bulgaria and 31 in Lithuania).

Of course, the size of the country is hardly the major factor for determining people's fears; nor can it be a reliable determinant of social and political processes taking place in society. For instance, several relatively small former communist countries in Europe such as Moldova, Romania, and Georgia were in a much worse economic and social situation than Russia and Ukraine. There are other factors that contributed to the differences among these countries.

For example, military industries played the dominant economic role in both Soviet Ukraine and Russia, which was not necessarily the case for Bulgaria and Lithuania. The difficulties during the demilitarization of the economy, and the conversion of the military industry were among major obstacles during the post-Soviet transformation. The difficulties that the governments in these countries experienced in their attempt to restructure the military-oriented industries may explain, in part, the differences in the unemployment level among these countries. The official level of unemployment in "big" countries was smaller than in the "small" nations: 3.4 percent of labor force in Russia and 1.5 in Ukraine against 11.1 and 7.1 in Bulgaria and Lithuania (The World Bank, 1999). It was remarkable that while the level of unemployment in Bulgaria and Lithuania was higher than in Russia and Ukraine, the fear of losing a job was higher in the "big" countries (78 percent in Ukraine and 61 percent in Russia, against 51 percent in Bulgaria and 53 percent in Lithuania). For Bulgarians and Lithuanians the status of unemployed was considered somewhat more "secure" than it was for Russians and Ukrainians.

These countries are also different in terms of the length of their tenure with communist regime. People in Russia and Ukraine lived under communism for more than seven decades, while in the small countries the duration was just about four decades. This circumstance could have influenced the process of adjustment to new social conditions: In the countries with the enduring traditions of communism, the transition should take place with more difficulties.

Finally, Ukraine and Russia were less socially homogenous than Bulgaria and Lithuania. To illustrate, in Ukraine, the richest 10 percent of the population were 37 times wealthier than the bottom 10 percent. In Russia, the same ratio was 27; in Bulgaria and Lithuania the indicators were 7 and 9 times respectively (World Bank, 1999).

In general, the frequency and intensity of fears expressed by Ukrainians was greater than in other countries in the studied sample. An attitude gap between Ukrainians and Lithuanians, for example, was 35 points in their assessment of their fear of "impoverishment." The gap was even greater regarding fear of "complete lawlessness." Only 39 percent of Lithuanians feared lawlessness in 1999, 40 points lower than Ukrainians. While only 10 percent of Russians (the lowest among the countries of the project) worried about "the end of this world," three times more Ukrainians (28 percent) reported this fear. Ukrainians also were "ahead" of all other studied samples in the frequency of expression of their fear of cosmic catastrophes and the eradication of life on earth (25 percent against 10 percent among Russians). Ukrainians were also more fearful than Russians in almost all categories.

Irrational Fears?

In the current project, there were two types of irrational fears examined among respondents in Russia, Ukraine, Bulgaria, and Lithuania: fear of the end of the world and fear about omnipotent domestic and international enemies. Among the fears of the first category were fears of "the end of this world" (the average was 17 percent in all countries), "annihilation of all people as a result of cosmic catastrophe" (17 percent), and the "seizure of power on the earth by aliens" (6 percent). The predominant fears in the second group were fears of "Masons and their attempt to seize the world" (8 percent) and "Zionist Jewish conspirators" (7 percent). More respondents in Ukraine reported the existence of such fears (16 percent) than in other countries: Bulgaria (12), Lithuania (9), and Russia (7). In general, irrational fears were not among the most salient worries in people of post-communist countries.

The study showed that many people in the examined countries held fatalistic and passive attitudes about dangers. When asked in a survey "What actions can you take to protect yourself against crimes?," 36 percent of the Russians said "nothing," compared to 18 percent of Bulgarians. The number of Russians who wanted to fight ecological problems, such as pollution, was even lower; only 39 percent of the Russians pledged to do something against 51 percent in Bulgaria. Polls show that passivity and fatalism of Russians increased during the 1990s (VTSIOM, *Monitoring Obshestvennogo Mnenia,* no. 4, 1999, p. 55).

Hopelessness is not a specific "ethnic" feature of the individual's personality. What makes people less hopeful or more optimistic—among many other factors—are social conditions to which people are currently exposed and the history of people's struggle for decent life. Moreover, social passivity is caused by disbelief in ability of the ordinary person, even with the help of others, to influence the situation in the country and in the government, which is by law obliged to guarantee protection against crime, impoverishment, and destruction of property. Social passivity has taken place in Lithuania as well, but to a lesser degree than in other countries of the former Soviet Union. One of the major things that Lithuanians have developed, however, is the unity of the nation, unity in struggle against the general adversary (the USSR and communism). Victory over "the invader" in the late 1980s has helped most people in Lithuania to further develop and keep something the Russians have not found yet—the national idea. Coupled with democratic values, this idea can consolidate millions of people of diverse interests and thus secure democracy.

Coping with Fears

Fear plays many regulatory roles in the individual's life. First, fears serve as signals. They warn the person about dangers and mobilize the person to aver such dangers (De Becker, 1997). On the other hand, fear, especially if it is persistent and supported by reasoning, may affect the person's single reactions and complex behavior. Fears of the similar type that develop in many individuals bring about feelings of uncertainty in society, which may have nefarious implications. Social psychologists call this phenomenon "self-fulfilling prophecy," referring to the attitudes and beliefs that people hold that "produce" the very outcomes that these individuals expect to find. In other words, a perceiver's fears about particular societal dangers may lead to that person behaving as if the threats really existed. Fear of crime and criminals, for instance, may provoke people to perform violent acts arguing that they are conducted in "self-protection." Fear of a conflict, in cases of self-fulfilling prophecy, may cause an escalation of the conflict.

The prevalence of particular fears may be an "opened gate" for populists and dictators who promise easy solutions and societal "shortcuts" for the sake of stability and fear reduction. History shows that the installation of a dictatorship almost always follows the proceeds by the spread of fears and anxiety among members of society. These fears may be justified, or they may be exaggerated. It does not matter, which way the process goes. What matters the most, though, is that there are political forces that are eager to speculate on people's fears to achieve these forces' political goals. Hitler's victory in 1933 was possible not only because of the poor economic conditions in Germany, but also because the Nazis were able to forment the fear of a disaster in the country.

Political rivals in the studied post-communist countries also used fears to achieve their political goals: collect as many "scared" votes as possible. Communists and left-wing parties intimidate people primarily by the threat of skyrocketing prices and unemployment. Their opposition from the right insists that ex-communist and other "left-wingers" will destroy democratic institutions and limit people's rights.

In economic life, fear of various "objective" negative developments, such as high inflation and economic depression affected human worries about their money and changed the consumer's behavior. In Russia, economic fears, which were primarily justified, worsened the economic situation even further because people refused to invest their money into Russian economy. Most people kept their money at home in hard currency. For example, in March 1999, people bought hard currency four times more than depositing their savings in banks or stock companies (*Statisticheskoie Obozrenie,* no. 2, 1999, p. 13). Many of those who could potentially make the best living and the biggest investments (professionals and talented young people) emigrated from the country.

The presence of fears in the minds of the people signals not only the quality of the life and the overall state of the economy. Fears also suggest that there is a psychological foundation of the direct threats to democratic institutions in these countries. A fearful person is more likely to accept political demagoguery of the radicals from either "left" or "right" flanks of the political spectrum. Fortunately for the post-communist countries, people's transitional fears did not influence any political and social consequences suggestive of the ongoing reverse from the democratic transformation. History shows, however, that human emotions can play a significant role in politics and no politician in the transitional country should believe that the road to authoritarianism, belligerent nationalism, or outbursts of populism is finally closed.

It is our intent to believe that although human fears are largely caused by certain events, persistent social problems, and economic difficulties, fear itself may become a powerful motivator of human behavior. By monitoring the dynamics of fears, we are able to have some insight in the direction of the historical processes for these as well as other countries in the world.

A Case Essay

American Fears: Change and Continuity

David W. Rohde

As a political scientist who studies American national politics I have a strong interest in the political consequences of public opinion and in the forces that cause public opinion to change or persist. In this brief note I want to discuss some of those forces and provide some evidence regarding American public opinion during the last forty years to illustrate and illuminate that discussion.

In democratic countries, the peoples' fears, concerns, or worries—whatever term we use—have substantial political relevance. Citizens expect their government (and the politicians that run it) to ameliorate, if not solve, the problems that give rise to these fears. Thus the fears of the people, and their evaluation of government's performance relative to them, have significant implications for politicians' survival in office. I will argue that the fears of the people are based in part on real enduring concerns about major issues in their lives, in part on more secondary issues, and in part on illusory matters stimulated by the media and politicians. We will take up each of these aspects in turn.

Dominant Concerns and Real-World Context

The main data I will draw on are survey responses to questions about what is the most important problem facing the United States at the time. This is not exactly the same as what people fear, but I think it is close enough for my purposes. The data come from two sources: The first is the set of National Election Studies (NES) conducted in presidential election years from 1972 to 1996 by the Survey Research Center - Center for political Studies of the University of Michigan (Abramson et al., 1999).

The NES data are broken down into four main categories (with some further refinement into subcategories): economics, social issues, foreign and defense, and functioning of government. The numbers show a close and easily comprehended link to changing circumstances in the real world. In 1972, the ongoing war in Vietnam was still a major issue, and fully 25 percent of the sample chose that as the most important issue (with other respondents choosing some other aspect of foreign and defense policy, bringing the total in that category to 34 percent). Yet only four years later, with the war ended, merely 4 percent of the sample selected some aspect of aspect of foreign and defense matters as most important. Then in 1980 and 1984, as the Cold War warmed up again during the Reagan administration and the United States pursued a major defense build up, about a third of the sample chose this issue. Then came the end of the Cold War, and foreign and defense policy receded into unimportance to the pubic.

Analogous, and even more striking, variations occurred with respect to economic matters. In 1972, the economy was perceived to be in relatively good shape, and so more respondents chose either social issues or foreign/defense matters as most important. Beginning with 1976, however, and in every election through 1992, the economy was chosen by more people than any other category as most important. (The specific aspect of the economy that people focused on varied, however. We will return to that matter later.) In 1976, both inflation and unemployment were problems and Jimmy Carter highlighted those issues in his campaign against President Ford. Then in 1980, with even worse economic numbers, Ronald Reagan turned the tables on Carter and triumphed. In 1984, Reagan had problems with the residue of a recession as well as the ballooning budget deficit, although he won handily anyway. Then, in 1988, Dukakis unsuccessfully tried to use the deficit as an issue to defeat Bush, while in 1992 Clinton focused on both unemployment and the budget and won. In five consecutive presidential elections, real (or perceived) economic problems were reflected in the concerns of the electorate, and the political campaigns highlighted those concerns in their strategies.

By contrast, in the 1996 election the public recognized that neither inflation nor unemployment was a serious problem, and the deficit situation was improving. Only 29 percent of respondents selected an economic issue as the most important problem—the lowest percentage since 1972—and Clinton won an easy victory. Indeed, nearly twice as many people chose a social issue as important, divided between social welfare (important mostly to Democrats) and public order (more important to Republicans). From election to election, the public's concerns vary, but in each case we can see a strong link between those concerns and important real problems in the country. In particular, when there are significant economic problems that are perceived to threaten the economic wellbeing of the people we can see that those concerns will dominate the public's perceptions and freeze out less serious and more ephemeral matters. Furthermore, it seems that it is more difficult for politicians to manipulate the saliency of these central issues or to draw attention away from them if there are real difficulties or to convince them that there is a problem without real-world support for the claim.

Better Times and Secondary Issues

If it is true that public concerns about major issues, such as the economy, are dominant and linked closely to real-world events, what happens when these major issues recede because conditions are perceived to be good? The evidence at hand seems to indicate that other matters come to the fore, and that public concerns about those issues tend to be rather volatile.

In the wake of the 1980 presidential election, the 1981 numbers show, for example, that concern about inflation dominated public attention, with a large portion of respondents (about one sixth) also worried about unemployment. Nothing else worried more than six percent of respondents. One year later, as America was gripped by the worst recession since the Great Depression, economic concerns still dominated, but the balance had shifted. Now fully 61 percent of respondents listed unemployment as the worst problem, with 18 percent citing inflation and 11 percent the economy in general. The same top priorities persisted into 1983, although finally one noneconomic concern reached the ten percent level.

By 1987, however, the state of the American economy had improved markedly. Both inflation and unemployment were down, and economic concerns only slightly outdistanced a new worry: drugs. The media, as well as certain politicians, had begun to focus public attention on drug use, especially among young people. From 1987 to 1989, as the state of the economy continued to be good, the proportion of people who listed drugs as their principal concern skyrocketed from 11 percent to 63 percent. Then, just as quickly, from 1989 to 1991, it fell back to 10 percent. Moreover, a large portion of the volatile shift in public concerns took place over a small fraction of that four-year period. The proportion of respondents indicating that drugs were the most important problem rose from 27 percent to 63 percent, and then back down to 38 percent—all between May and November of 1989.

It is beyond the scope of this brief note to offer an analysis of the specific political events or journalistic coverage that were related to the rise and decline of public concerns about drugs that are indicated by the data. It is sufficient to recognize that it is implausible that there was real change in the level of drug use during the four years from 1987 to 1991 (much less from May to November of 1989) to provide a basis for these fluctuating opinions. It is also worth noting that these changes occurred without the rise of other major issues to displace drugs in the public's mind. Instead public concern with the economy or anything else never rose above 10 percent during 1989, and, even in the longer period from 1987 to 1991, no other issue surpassed 20 percent.

Returning to the time series, some economic uncertainties coupled with the effects of the ongoing presidential campaign lead to the renewal of public concern over the economy in 1992. More than a third of the sample cited the economy in general as a problem, and 27 percent specifically mentioned unemployment. This new focus on economic issues blanketed other concerns, with no other problem exceeding 7 percent. Then by early 1994 the economy had again improved. Only 17 percent of respondents mentioned general economic concerns, so other, more transitory issues, came to the fore. This time it was the crime problem, which was named by a majority of the sample. As with the previous situation with drugs, there is no plausible evidence that real increases in the level of crime in the United States lay behind this jump in public concern. It is clear, however, that politicians—particularly Republicans—sought to raise the saliency of this issue among the public because they believed that they could gain electoral advantage from it. This also was clearly one of the issues that helped the Republicans gain a majority in the House of Representatives in the 1994 elections (Jacobson, 1995).

To recapitulate the point of this section, when the dominant real concerns of the public are largely satisfied, less important issues that may be less well-grounded in real world events may come to the fore, and their prominence may be due to the focusing effect of media and politicians. The corollary is that if the central concerns, like the economy, again become salient, these more transitory concerns will recede in prominence.

More Illusory Concerns

As a final category, we may take note of a more extreme instance of the type discussed in the previous section: public fears that are not well grounded in the situations in the world around us. As I have argued, the saliency of certain issues to people, and peoples' attitudes about those issues, can be influenced by the actions of media and politicians. The media may choose to allocate a relatively large amount of coverage to events because they are dramatic and are expected to be interesting to their target audience. Analogously, politicians may choose to speak extensively and often about an issue because they believe that by doing so they can enhance their political position with the public. These activities focus public attention on the issue and can raise the saliency of the issue in the minds of voters. (In the political psychology literature, this effect has been labeled "priming.") The point of this for our present purposes is that such effects can create a distorted public perception of the reality about the issue.

A salient example of this can be drawn from recent U.S. experience. In April of 1999, a horrendous mass killing occurred at Columbine High School in Littleton Colorado, followed by the suicide of the two perpetrators. In addition, a number of other shootings occurred in schools around that time. Understandably, these events drew a lot of attention from the media and from politicians. The events themselves were covered extensively, with numerous follow-up stories seeking explanations and reactions. There were also legislative hearings that looked for causes and solutions. The theory of priming would expect that this focusing of attention would lead the public to see the issue of school safety as increasingly important, and also that people would come to perceive the problem of school violence to be more prevalent than they had previously. This would occur, moreover, regardless of whether the perception was in accord with reality.

This appears to have been the case. Public concern about school safety increased markedly. The percentage of parents who feared for the safety of their students in school rose from 24 percent in 1977, to 37 percent in 1998, and 55 percent in 1999 (Henry, 2000). Justice Department statistics showed that in the late 1990s, the percentage of students who feared being attacked in school also rose. In the wake of this, programs designed to reduce the occurrence of school violence were instituted all across the country. Yet data show that schools are one of the safest places for children to be. "Education Department statistics . . . show school crime has decreased in the past five years and that there's a million-to-one chance of a student being a homicide victim. Ninety percent of schools don't have any serious violent crime. . . ." (Henry 2000: p. 2D). Indeed, data from the National School Safety Center showed that deaths on school grounds in 1999–2000 were down from 1995–96. In addition, the percentage of students who reported bringing a weapon to school at least one day in the previous thirty days had dropped from 12 percent in 1993, to 10 percent in 1995, and 8 percent in 1997.

Of course, these facts do not in any way mitigate the horror of the school killings that occurred, nor do they indicate a defect in the parents and students who reacted with concern. They do illustrate, however, that while some public opinions are the direct result of accurate perceptions about real-world events, other attitudes can misperceive reality, and this can happen because of media focus or political activity. It is likely, on the other hand, that concerns and opinions like these will be less enduring than those founded more firmly on reality.

Supply-Side and Demand-Side Influences on Public Fears

The last point I want to make is to emphasize a perspective that has been implicit in the discussion. That is that public opinions in general, and fears in particular, are affected by (to use current terminology from political science) both "demand-side" and "supply-side" forces. In this context, demand-side influences would include people's enduring attitudes and the events in the world that they directly experience. So when the economy goes into a deep recession, or when inflation sharply rises, or when a terrorist act is committed, people can see the effects in their environment and they react to those effects. But supply-side influences are different. They are the result of actions by elites, including politicians and people in the media, which are intended to serve the interests of those elites. The effects on people's fears and concerns may be merely byproducts, as when the media focuses heavily on a dramatic issue in order to increase the public's attention to them. Here the motive is increasing the profit of the media outlet or the celebrity of the reporter, and the enhancing of public concern is not a deliberate intent.

On the other hand, the shift in public fears may be by design, as when an ambitious politician who is identified with an issue position seeks to increase its saliency in order to enhance his or her support. In either case, it is important for us as analysts to recognize that the public opinions that we study are not always only the consequence of peoples enduring attitudes and their unfiltered experiences. They can also be influenced by the actions of other actors, and those actors have their own motives and goals. This fact has, I believe, important implications for the "shape" of public opinion, and even more important implications for our interpretations of those opinions and our expectations about their continuity and change.

A Case Essay

Fears in Ex-Soviet Union Immigrants in Israel

V. Aptekman

The last decade of the twentieth century—the fifth from the date of the foundation of Israel—has been marked by, unprecedented in the entire history of the country, and oversize flow of immigration, mostly from the republics of the ex-Soviet Union. The population of the state increased by nearly a million people. It is no wonder that this augmentation resulted in important changes in both the economic and the social structures and in the overall cultural and moral climate of the country in general.

For the individual, immigration is the breaking of certain stereotypes. One has to reject the "old" life standards and to face new difficulties, which may vary from the linguistic barriers and professional hurdles to the puzzles of everyday life and climatic adaptations. In spite of the fact that immigration to Israel is considered "repatriation," the problems that people face remain the same. Moreover, many of the difficulties, which new repatriates have to deal with in the first days and often years of their "new" life, are more complex than immigrants face in many other countries. This situation is partially due to the limited economic and other opportunities of a very small country troubled by ethnic tensions. Although Israel officially is regarded as a Jewish state where all Jews become a part of the melting pot of Israeli culture, in reality there are two major population groups: "the ashkenazi" and "the Sephardim." These two groups have lived in isolation from each other for many centuries, and up to the present time hold onto their own lifestyles and traditions and do not truly mix into the cultural melting pot. Moreover, there is a significant cultural variation within the immigrant population on the basis of origin from different ethnic regions of the former U.S.S.R. For example, the Jews from the republics of Central Asia and Georgia, were less assimilated into their former cultures than the Jews from the European part of former USSR, especially from big cities such as Moscow, Leningrad, Riga, or Minsk. As a group, the former are more religious and feel themselves closer to the Jewish traditions than their European counterparts.

It is very important to look at the issues facing the immigrants in the context of Israeli social and political situation in general. The legacy of numerous conflicts and war in this region can not be erased. One of many problems is the uncertainty of the future of the West Bank territories and the Golan Heights. For many years, Israel remains in the state of war and this contributes to numerous security problems. Therefore, most of the new immigrants find themselves faced with the necessity of adjusting to a life in constant danger, which should influence people's perception of reality and affect their fears. The degree of the immigrant's awareness of this situation varies and is linked to the duration of residency in the country, the age and social status of the individual, and the place of residence. For this research, six major cities were selected, which varied according to their geographic location, political role, and socioeconomic conditions: Jerusalem, Kiriat-Arba, Khadera, Netania, Haifa, and Arad.

Among the Jews of the Diaspora, Jerusalem is regarded not only as the political capital of Israel but also as the spiritual center of the Jewish nation. At the same time, a big part of the city is dominated by Arab population. Furthermore, Jerusalem is one of the poorest cities in the country. Kiriat Arba is one of the biggest Jewish settlements on the West Bank territories, located beyond the so-called "green line." It borders the Arab town of Hebron inhabited mostly by Muslim Palestinian population. The cities of the central part of the country (Tel Aviv, Netania, and Khadera) belong to the most developed region of the state and are considered relatively secure. The city of Haifa, famous for being the center of the country's heavy industry, is also known for its traditionally "leftist" electorate. The city is bi-national, has a considerable percentage of Christian Arab population, and the relations between the Jewish and the Arab population are known to be relatively peaceful. It is also important to stress that Haifa has second to Tel Aviv area the largest percentage of the immigrant population. The southern regions of the country are represented by the city of Arad, a small town in the Negev desert. Arad's population consists of a large percentage of immigrants from the big cities of Russia, such as Moscow and St. Petersburg, who are mostly 50 years of age and older. Although well-developed and with good infrastructure, Arad has a large unemployment rate, a feature characteristic of Israeli developing cities.

People emigrate because many of them want to escape from the past and they are driven by the hope for the future. Among the major reasons for emigration from the Soviet Union and Russia were the instability of political situation in the country, ethnic and religious discrimination, the absence of positive professional prospects, and fears for themselves and the future of the children. The main question of the subsequent research conducted in Israel was to determine whether emigration alleviated the fears and resolved the problems from the past, and more importantly, whether it was conducive to the formation of self-confidence in the people who decided to emigrate.

The results of the survey revealed the following. To the question, "How confident are you of your future prospects?," 18 percent of the respondents expressed their complete confidence, some confidence was expressed by 42 percent, 21 percent were somewhat not confident, and 6 percent were absolutely not confident in their future. The evaluation of the answers according to the demographic criteria revealed that the answers depend strongly on the age and gender of the respondent. For example, there was a gap between men in women: Female respondents tend to be the least confident of their future, while males are more confident.

The most confident in their future are also young men, who have just finished their three years in the military service in the Israeli Army. One of the possible explanations for this gap—aside from the "natural" optimism of the young—is that in Israel, the individual's service in the army traditionally leads to a greater chance for a successful career. The answers provided by respondents further reveal that older people, in general, seem to be less confident of the future than the younger generation. Also the least confident are the people with advanced degrees of college education and highly qualified specialists. The reason for this is that in the context of Israeli economy, these people's qualifications and professional potential often remain unrealized. Upon entering the job market they often find themselves overqualified and are forced to change their profession to one requiring a different set of skills, which often does not reflect their educational abilities.

The answers to the question about the main area of the respondents' worries were distributed relatively evenly (34 to 38 percent) among the following for categories: relatives, children, oneself, and the future of Israel. It is interesting that in a study of pre-emigrants conducted in Russia, among the answers to a similar question worries about children were dominant and served as one of the main reasons for emigration. However, in the research conducted in Israel, people who were most concerned about the future of their children were from the families in which the mother was not Jewish. This worry is reflective of the problems of those people who are not regarded as Jews according to the orthodox Jewish law. Although these people do have Israeli citizenship and equal educational and professional opportunities, they often encounter bureaucratic barriers in civil procedures, such as obtaining official permission for burial or marriage.

Overall, the political situation in the region determines the direction and extent of the immigrants' fears. Only 8 percent of the questioned individuals responded that they are not worried at all abut the political situation in the country. For example, most people in the sample mentioned the fear that arises from the threat of possible terrorist attacks: More than 61 percent of the respondents answered that they feel "permanent anxiety and strong fear" of terrorism. The degree of fears of terrorism depends on the place where the respondent lives. For example, in Jerusalem the number of people who mentioned this fear is 12 percent higher than in the overall sample. Young people who have completed their military service take the problem with more composure, while the older people tend to feel permanent fear and thread.

The danger of the possible creation of the Palestinian state is in the second place on the list of possible dangers: fifty-one percent of the respondents mentioned about their "permanent anxiety and strong fear" of Palestinian independence. For many citizens, especially of right-wing orientations, the proposed Arab state is regarded as hostile and intended to destroy the Jewish state of Israel. In contrast to the respondents' perception of the terrorist threats, fear of the formation of the Palestinian state does not depend on the region in which the respondent resides. The distribution of answers is the same for Jerusalem and Kiriat Arba, which could become a part of Palestinian territory, and for Netania and Haifa which, on the other hand, will remain in Israel.

Economic problems contribute to the immigrant population's overall concerns and fears. The growing unemployment is a cause of fear appeared in 74 percent of the answers. According to our data, among the people who left the former USSR between 1990 to 1992, more than two thirds had a professional or a university degree. Upon their arrival to Israel, many of these people had to descend a few steps in the socioeconomic hierarchy. The major reason for this situation is found in the Israeli economic situation in general. Because of scarcity of jobs, many of the incoming specialists are overqualified and cannot find occupation according to their education and experience. According to the answers of the majority of the respondents, only 26 percent do not feel constant anxiety about their professional future or their economic prospects. Many respondents are worried about the possible, probable, or already existing loss of their professional qualifications.

Bureaucratization and corruption of the social and political systems are among other problems that the immigrant population mentions as causing anxiety and fears. It is obvious that an immigrant, a newcomer without a good knowledge of the local language and culture, suffers more from the bureaucratic system than a person who has lived in the country for many years and knows how the system is operated. Almost 80 percent of the respondents expressed worry about the bureaucracy. In addition, immigrants expressed their worries about their inability to read business and other official documents (58 percent) and said that they fear the Israeli bureaucratic machine.

The danger of the growing orthodox influence may result, as noted by the respondents, in the restraining of modern sciences, cultural censorship, the suppression of non-Jewish or mixed population, and general domination of religious norms on secular culture. One of the examples of suppression at present is the fact that in Jerusalem the public celebration of the year 2000 (a Christian date, according to Jewish Orthodox beliefs) was officially forbidden.

The wish to live in a Jewish state and be able to keep their own Jewish traditions were among the main reasons for people's emigration from their home countries. However, emigration has brought forward fears of a possible loss of cultural identity without acquiring a new one in a new country. Nearly 36 percent of respondents expressed "some worry" or "some regrets" about this possible loss. This fear is present mostly among the natives of big cultural centers such as Moscow, St. Petersburg, Minsk, Riga, and Kiev, where the degree of assimilation was higher than in small towns. For many formerly Russian Jews a cultural tradition they grew upon was Russian, Ukrainian, etc., and not necessarily Jewish tradition. The lack of fluency in Hebrew and the gap between ethnic groups within both the Israeli and the immigrant communities leaves Russian immigrants with a fear that they may be left outside the mainstream Israeli culture. The anxiety of such a possibility is reflected by 16 percent of total respondents.

The final group of factors contributing to anxiety includes the problems of the general moral situation in the world: the future of life on the planet and the changing moral and cultural values of civilization in general. Among the general problems which cause worry or anxiety, the fear of growing materialism and the loss of spiritual values are mentioned most often. In general, this group of concerns occupies the last place on the scale of the causes for fear and anxiety. Nearly all the respondents reject this group as a possible cause for distress.

Despite the fact that the majority of the problems that preoccupy the Russian immigrants in Israel are pertinent to their new life in Israel, the remaining strong cultural connection with the former USSR results in a continuous cultural and psychological ties with the ex-homeland. Russian immigrants get their information about the present situation in Russia through several channels: cable television, Russian-speaking radio and newspapers, friends and relatives, and personal visits. Problems of contemporary Russia and other countries of the former USSR continue to distress the new Russian Israelis.

References

Abramson, P. and Inglehart, R. (1995). *Value Change in Global Perspective,* Ann Arbor: University of Michigan Press.

Abramson, P., Aldrich, J., and Rohde, D. (1999). *Change and Continuity in the 1996 and 1998 Elections.* Washington, D.C.: CQ Press.

Agence France Presse (2000). "Israel Embassy Pulls out of Belarus over Radioactivity Fears." Press release. May 19.

American Jewish Committee (1998). *Annual Survey of American Jewish Opinion,* NY, pp.1–2.

AP (Associated Press) (1996) International News Russian Poll: "Fears of Chernobyl-Like Disaster Widespread," April 25.

Babosov, E. M. *Chernobyl'skaya tragediya v ee sotsial'nyh izmereniyah.* Minsk: Pravo I Economika, 1996; F. Maysenya (ed.), *Chernobyl': chelovecheskoe izmerenie.* Belarus Monitor. Special Issue. April 1996. Minsk: National Center for Strategic Initiatives "Vostok-Zapad."

Bandazevsky, J. (1999). "Opozdala vsya Belarus." *Belorusskaya Delovaya Gazeta,* 26 April.

Baltic News Service (1995). *Lithuanians Know about AIDS but Don't Think They Will Be Infected.* October 2.

Baltic News Service (2000). *Euro-integration support up in Lithuania.* April 19.

Baltic News Service (2000). *Fifty Percent of Lithuanians Would Sell their Land to Anyone Regardless of Buyers' Nationality.* August 1.

Basina, Y. (1998). Nekotorye aspekty problemy individualisma i kollektivisma v rossiyskom obschestvennom soznanii: Differentsiatsii i edinstvo. In *Chelovek v perekhodnom obshchestve. Sotsiologicheskiye n sotsialno-psikhologicheskiye issledovaniya.* Moscow, p. 91.

Belapan News Agency (2000). Excerpt from report. Minsk, August 4.

BNS Baltic News Agency (1999). *Speaker Tells Estonian Premier of Concern over Anti-Western Attitudes.* December 3.

Bobinski, C. and Robinson, A. (1993). "Poles' Fear of Future Obscures Past." *Financial Times.* September 8, p. 3.

Bolce, L. and De Maio, G. 1999. "Religious Outlook, Culture War Politics, and Antipathy toward Christian Fundamentalists. *Public Opinion Quarterly.* 63: 29–61.

Boski, P. (1991). O dwoch wymiarach lewicy-prawicy na scenie politycznej i w wartosciach politycznych polskich wyborców. In J. Reykowski (ed.), Wartosci i postawy społeczne a zmiany systemowe. Warszawa: IP PAN, pp. 49–105.

Burbulis, V. (1999). *Unemployment Main Problem for Lithuanians.* ITAR-TASS, November 15.

Butyrsky, Z. (1997). "Ukraine as NATO's information territory." *Segodnya,* p. 3.

Clover, C. and Hargreaves, D. (2000). "Solana Delivers Tough Message on Belarus Poll." *Financial Times* (London), July 22, p. 9.

Crossette, B. (1999). "Happiness, by the Numbers," *New York Times,* September 19.

Czapinski, J. (1996). "Uziemienie polskiej duszy." In M. Marody, E. Gucwa–Lesny (eds.). *Podstawy ?ycia społecznego w Polsce.* Warszawa: ISS, pp. 252–275.

Czapinski, J. (2000). "Jak rządzic narodem malkontentow." *Gazeta Wyborcza,* 12–13 Sierpnia.

Czuma, L. (1993). *Katolicka Nauka Spoleczna* (Catholic Social Science). Lublin: Katolicki Uniwersytet Lubelski.

Data files of the project "Catastrophes–98" in the OCA and SPSS formats (1998). The Constitution of the Population of Ukraine According to Sex and Ages, on the 1st January, 1996.

Davies, J. C. (1997). "Toward a Theory of Revolution." In J. C. Davies. *When Men Revolt and Why.* Transaction Publishers, New Brunswick, NJ, p. 134–148.

De Becker, G. (1997). *The Gift of Fears. Survival Signals that Protect us From Violence,* Boston: Little, Brown and Co.

De Tocqueville (1997). "How the Spirit of Revolt was Promoted by Well Intentioned Efforts to Improve the People's Lot." In J. C. Davies: *When Men Revolt and Why.* Transaction Publishers, New Brusnwick, NJ., p. 134–148.

Derczynski, W. (1998). "Opinie o Przyczynach Bezrobocia i Bezrobotnych." [Opinions on Reasons of Unemployment and Unemployed]. CBOS 12, 91–114.

Deutsche Presse-Agentur (2000). "Poles, Czechs, Hungarians Complain of Bad Government." Press release. August 10.

Diligensky, G. (1997). "Chto My Znayem o Demokratii i Grazdanskom Obschestve.' [What We Know about Democracy and Civil Society]. *Pro et Contra,* fall, p. 5–21.

Diligensky, G. (1998). "Rossiyskiy Gorozhanin Kontsa Devyanostyh: Genesis Postsovetskogo Soznaniya." [Russian City Resident of the Late Ninetieth: Genesis of Post-Soviet Reflection]. A manuscript. Moscow.

DINAU News Agency (1999). A quote from Chairman of the Ukrainian Supreme Council parliament, Oleksandr Tkachenko Kiev, February 3.

Dragohrust, Y. (1999). "Lozungi Integracii Upali v Cene." [Slogan of Integration Dropped in Value]. *Belorusskaya Delovaya Gazeta,* 4 May 1999.

Dubrovin, A. (1999). "Tihaya Okkupaciya Pod Grohot Barabanov." [Quiet Occupation Under the Rumble of Drums]. *Naviny,* 21 January.

Economist (1996). "Alexander the Not-So-Great." April 13, p. 42.

Ellsworth, P. and Gross, S. (1994). "Hardening of Attitudes: Americans' Views on the Death Penalty. *Journal of Social Issues,* 50, 2: 19–52.

Engelberg, S. (1991). "Polish State Keeps its Distance from Church." *The New York Times.* 26 May, section 4, p. 5.

Erikson, E. (1950). *Childhood and Society.* New York: Norton.

Erikson, E. (1968.) *Identity: Youth and Crisis.* New York: Norton.
ESP (1997). Ekonomicheskiye i sotsyalnye peremeny . . . 1997, no. 2, p. C. 79, 86; no. 3. p. 79.
Eurasia Economic Outlook. Washington, DC: WEFA Group, 1999, 6.22–6.23.
Falkowska, M. (1999). *Prestiz zawodow.* [Prestige of professions]. *CBOS* 3, 85–97.
Falkowska, M. (2000). *Egalitaryzm w społeczenstwie polskim* [Egalitarianism in Polish Society]. *CBOS* 2, 63–77.
Feduta, A. (2000). "Papa Is No Longer Trying to Butt in." *Moskovskiye Novosti,* no. 19, 16–22 May, p. 12.
Feierabend, I. K., Feierabend, R. L. and Nesvold, B. A. (1972). "Social Change and Political Violence: Cross-National Patterns" (p. 107–124). In Feierabend, I. K., Feierabend, R. L. and Gurr, T. R. (eds.) *Anger, Violence, and Politics. Theories and Research.* Prentice-Hall: Englewood Cliffs, NJ.
Ferguson, G. (1999). *Public Opinion in Ukraine 1999.* Washington, DC: IFES.
Gaidys V. (1996). "Political, Party Preferences and Political Identities in Lithuania." In *Changes of Identity in Modern Lithuania.* Social Studies 2, ed. M. Taljunaite. Vilnius: Institute of Philosophy and Sociology Republic of Lithuania, University of Goteborg, pp. 77–103 (1,5a.l.).
Gaidys V. (1996). "Attitudes Towards the Past, Present and Future in the Baltic States: 1993–1995." *Journal for Mental Changes. Perspectives of Economic, Political and Social Integration.* vol. II, no 1.
Gaidys V. and Tureikyte D. (1993). "Agoral Gatherings in Lithuania: An Example of The Baltic Way." In *Protection of Environment: Mental Changes and Social Integration Perspective.* Ed. Biela A. Lublin. Central European Centre for Behavioural Economics, pp. 85–90.
Galperin, M. (1996). "Redeeming the Captive. Twenty-Five Years of Successful Resettlement and Acculturation of New Americans." *Journal of Jewish Communal Service.* vol.72, no.4, Summer, p.229.
GKSR (1997). *Rossiiskii Statisticheskii Ezhegodnik,* Goskomizdat: Moscow.
Glassner, B. (1999). *The Culture of Fear: Why Americans Are Afraid of the Wrong Things,* New York: Basic Books.
Golovachev, V. (2000). "Worst of all Are Confusion and Chaos." *Trud,* 29 September.
Golovaha, Y. and Panina, N. (1999). "Protestniy Potencial Ukrainskogo Ibshestva," [Protest Potential of Ukrainian Society]. *Sotis,* 1999, no. 10: 31–40.
Goode, E. and Ben-Yehuda, N. (1994). *Moral Panics,* Oxford: Blackwell.
Gucwa-Lesny, E. (1996). "Zmiany Poziomu Zycia i Ich Ocena." In M. Marody, E. Gucwa-Lesny (eds.) *Podstawy Zycia Społecznego w Polsce,* Warszawa: ISS, pp.100–115.
Gudkov, L. and Levinson, A. (1994). "Attitudes Toward Jews." *Sociological Research,* March-April 1994.
Hannon, B. (2000). "CzeX-Files: Polls Reveal the Mystical Side." *The Prague Post;* 11 October.
Henry, T. (2000). "Scared at School." *USA Today,* 4 April: 1D.
Holley, D. (1999). "Long-admired Czech President Vaclav Havel Falls from Grace: Critics Appear To Be Pushing for the Czech Republic President to Step Aside." *The Vancouver Sun,* 6 February: A 15.

Holos Ukrayiny (1999). "Foreign Minister Tarasyuk Criticizes EU policy on Ukraine." November 23.

IBRD (1999). The International Bank for Reconstruction and Development, World Bank: Washington, pp. 46–48.

Interfax Russian News (2000). "Over 25 Percent of Russians Fear Chernobyl-style Accident Could Occur Again." Moscow: 24 April.

Interfax Russian News (1999). A press release. Moscow: 26 February.

Interfax Russian News (1999). "Seventy-Two Percent of Russians Support Union With Belarus." 28 May.

Interfax Russian News (2000). A press release. Kiev: 11 April.

Interfax-Ukraine (1998). A press release. Kiev: 29 July.

Interfax-Ukraine (2000). A press release. Kuev: 11 April.

ITAR-TASS (1998). A press release. Moscow: 1 October.

Ivanova, V. and Shubkin, V. (1999). " Struktura Strakhov I Trevog v Rossii I na Ukraine." [Structure of Feaers and Anxiety in Russia and Ukraine]. *Mir Rossii,* n. 1–2.

IVVM–Mišovič, J. (2000a). *Názory na Vztahy se Sousedními Zeměmi, Zejména Rakouskem.* [Opinions on Relations with Neighboring Countries, Namely Austria], 20 March.

IVVM–Mišovič, J. (2000b). *Ke 150. Výročí Narození T. G. Masaryka.* [On the Occasion of the 150th Anniversary of Masaryk's Birthday], 26 April.

IVVM–Rezková, M., (2000a). *Jaké Prolémy Zneklidňují Občany.* [What Problems Worry Citizens], 1 June.

IVVM–Rezková, M. (2000b). *Veřejnost o Ekologii.* [The Public on Ecology], 13 June.

IVVM–Rezková, M., (2000c). *Hodnocení Oplynulého Roku, Očekávání do Budoucna.* [Evaluation of the Past year, Future Expectations], 24 January.

IVVM–Jelínek, V. (2000). *Postoje občanů k otázce imigrace.* [Attitudes of Citizens toward the Immigrant Issue], 12 June.

Izgarshev, I. and Zaks, A. (1999). "Strashno li Segodnia Zhit v Stolitse?" [Is it Scary Today to Live in the Capital?] *Argumenty i Fakty,* no. 40, p. 21.

Jacobson, G. (1995). "The 1994 House Elections in Perspective." In Philip A. Klinker (ed). *Midterm: Elections of 1994 in Context.* Boulder, Colorado: Westview Press, pp. 1–20.

Jakubowska, U. (1999a). *Preferencje polityczne. Psychologiczne teorie i badania* [Political preferences. Psychological theories and research]. Warszawa: IP PAN.

Jakubowska, U. (1999b). "Approval for Politicians and Political Ideas: Who Supports Whom and Why?" *Journal for Mental Change* 5: 65–86.

Jalowiecki, B. (1996). "Kwestie regionalne." In M. Marody and E. Gucwa-Lesny (eds.). *Podstawy Zycia Społecznego w Polsce,.* Warszawa: ISS, pp. 302–323.

Kapelyushny, L. (1996). "Ten Years with Chernobyl." *Izvestia,* 25 April, p. 5.

Kapustin, A. (1997). "Debate on the Results of Yeltsin's Visit." *Nezavisimaya Gazeta.* 19 June, p. 3.

Karbalevich, V. (1999). "Belarus: Raskolotoe obshestvo." [Belarus: A Divided Society] *Belorusskaya Delovaya Gazeta,* 5 April.

Kelley, H. (1967). "Attribution Theory in Social Psychology." In D. Levine (ed.). *Nebraska symposium of motivation.* Lincoln, NB: University of Nebraska Press, Vol. 15, pp. 192–240.

Kesselman L. and Matskevich M. (1998). "Individual Optimism/Pessimism in the Contemporary Russian Transformation." *Sociology: Theory, Methods, Marketing,* no. 1–2. p. 164–175.

Khandohiy, V. (2000). Quoted by *Fakty i Kommentari.* "New Head of Mission to NATO Favors Closer Cooperation." 12 May.

Kirkpatrick, J. (1991). "Democracy Seen as Best Choice." *The Financial Post* (Toronto). 13 May, p. 10.

Klicperová, M., Feierabend, I. K., and Hofstetter, C. R., (1997a). "In the Search of a Post-Totalitarian Syndrome: A Theoretical Framework and Empirical Assessment." *Journal of Community and Applied Social Psychology,* 7 (1): 39–52.

Klicperová, M., Feierabend, I.K., Hofstetter, C. R:, (1997b). "Peaceful Conflict Resolution in Czechoslovakia." In K. Bjorkqvist and D. P. Fry (eds.). *Cutlural Variations in Conflict Resolution: Alternatives to Violence.* Lawrewnce Erlbaum Associates, Mahwah, NJ.

Klicperová-Baker, M., Feierabend, I. K., Hofstetter, C. R. (1999a). "Post-Communist Syndrome." (pp. 161–184). In M. Klicperová-Baker, *Ready for Democracy? Civic Culture and Civility with a Focus on Czech Society.* Institute of Psychology, Academy of Sciences of the Czech Republic, Prague.

Klicperová-Baker, M., Feierabend, I. K., Hofstetter, C. R., et al. (1999b). "Czech Democratic Heritage and Present Youth." (pp. 57–84). In. M. Klicperová-Baker, *Ready for Democracy? Civic Culture and Civility with a Focus on Czech Society.* Institute of Psychology, Academy of Sciences of the Czech Republic, Prague.

Kondratenko, N. (1995). "Most of Moscow, St.Petersburg Residents Say Fascism Fears are Grounded." ITAR-TASS, 14 April.

Kolarska-Bobinska, L. (1997). Konsolidacja demokracji w Polsce. In: L. Kolarska-Bobińska, A. Markowski (eds.). *Prognozy i Wybory. Polska demokracja* 1995 (11–32). Warszawa: Wydawnictwo Sejmowe.

Kostikov, V. (1999). "Revkiem Dlia Rodiny" [Requiem for Motherland]. *Nezavisimaia Gazeta,* 2 February.

Koblanski, B. (1996). "Poles Fear Foreigners Buying Land." *Nowa Europa,* 11 June p. 17.

Kučerová, R. (1998). "Interpersonal Relations." Diploma thesis. Department of Sociology, Karlova Universita, Prague.

Latsis, O. (1995.) "Sovietskaia tsivilizatsia unikal'na. I v etom nasha beda," [Soviet Civilization is Unique. And this is Our Misfortune]. *Izvestia,* 12 April.

Levada, Y. (1999a). "Opiat' drugim putem" [Again a New Way] *Vremia MN,* 26 October.

Levada, Y. (1999b). "Chelovek Sovetskiy: Desyat Let Spustya: 1989–1999." [The Soviet Man: Ten Years Later). *Monitoring,* 3, p.7–16.

Levada, Y. (1999c). Fenomen Vlasti v Obschestvennom Mnenii: Paradoksy i Stereotipy Vospriyatiya. [Phenomenon of Power in Public Opinion: Paradoxes and Stereotypes of Perception]. *Monitoring Obschestvennogo Mneniya,* no. 4, p. 9–15.

Levada, Y. (1999d). *Research Program Homo Sovieticus-III.* Unpublished manuscript.

Levinson, D. (1978). *The Seasons of a Man's Life.* New York: Knopf.

Maheshwari, V. and Robinson, A. (2000). "Pre-EU States Shuffle off their Soviet Past." *Financial Times* (London), 19 May, p. 1.

Markowski, R. (1997). "Spoleczne a polityczne podzialy spoleczenstwa polskiego." in: L. Kolarka-Bobinska, R. Markowski (eds.). *Prognozy i Wybory. Polska demokracja* 1995 (31–68). Warszawa: Wydawnictwo Sejmowe.

Martinovich, V. (1999) "V Minske sostoyalsya Chernobyl'skiy shlyah," *Belorusskaya Delovaya Gazeta,* 26 April.

Maslow, A. (1970). *Motivation and Personality.* Harper and Row, NY.

McCathie, A. (1996). "Czechs Facing Tough Economic Decisions After Elections." *Deutsche Presse-Agentur,* 30 May.

McKinsey, K. (1994). "Russian Muscle-Flexing Revives Fear in Poland." *The Ottawa Citizen.* 25 January, p. A6.

Melnik, M. (1998). "Most Ukrainians Want to Join Russia-Byelorussia Union." ITAR-TASS News Agency, March 5.

Monitoring Obshchestvennogo Mneniaa (1999). no. 3, p. 66.

Morawski, W. (1996). "Demokratyzacja. Od pragnien do Dostosowan." In M. Marody, E. Gucwa-Lesny (eds.). *Podstawy Zycia Społecznego w Polsce* (132–162). Warszawa: ISS.

New Democracies Barometer (1996). A study conducted by the Paul Lazarsfeld Society, Vienna. Centre for the Study of Public Policy, University of Strathclyde.

Nezavisimaya Gazeta (1996). "Belarusians Believe Elimination of USSR Was a Mistake." 10 February, p. 1.

Nikolaychuk, N. (1999). "Belorusy Vybirayut Geroin." [Belarusians Elect Heroines]. *Imya,* 30 April.

Novoprudsky, S. (2000). "The End of the CIS." *Izvestia,* 17 June 17.

Ogonyok (1998). "Poll: 56 Percent of Russians Think Russians and Ukrainians are a Single People." no. 7 (February), p. 29.

Opinion Analysis (1999). "Belarusians Endorse Union with Russia, Express Mistrust of NATO and the US." 4 August, p. 1.

Oreshkin, D. (1998). "Vybory v Rossii Vo Vremena El Nino" [Russian Electiond During El Nino]. *Rossiiskii Telegraf,* 23 April.

Orlova, R. (1983). *Memoirs,* New York: Random House

Panshina, N. (1998). "38 percent of Russians Favor Unification with Byelorussia." ITAR-TASS News Agency, 19 May.

Pankowski, K. (1999a). "Czy Warto Było Zmieniac Ustroj–Opinie Czechow, Wegrow i Polakow" [Was it Worth to Change Political System–Opinions of Czechs, Hungarians and Poles]. *CBOS,* 11, 5–8.

Pankowski, K. (2000). "Szczęsliwcy, Zzy Pechowcy? Samopoczucie Psychiczne Polakow w 1999 roku" [Lucky or unlucky people? Mental conditions of Poles in 1999]. *CBOS* 1, 44–58.

PAP News Wire (1999). "Christian Democrats: Lithuania Does not Observe Human Rights." 9 September.

PolitRu (1999). "Pravye o Soyuze s Belorussiey." [The Right about a Union with Belarus]. 27 October.

POR—*The Public Opinion Report* (2000). March 24, n. 11, p. 37.

Prince, S. (1920). *Catastrophe and Social Change, Based upon a Sociological Study of the Halifax Disaster,* New York: Columbia University Press.

Public Opinion Foundation (1998). Survey Reports Series, 16 Sep. n. 88, p. 28.

Rakowski, M. F. (1998). *Dzienniki Polityczne 1958–1962.* Warszawa: Iskry.

Ratnasabapathy, S. (1994). "Russia-Politics: Poll Shows Russians Would Shun Fascist Leader." *Inter Press Service,* April 26.

Reeves, P. (1996). "All Power to Europe's Dictator: Vote in Belarus Kills Democracy." *The Independent.* 26 November, p. 13.

Reykowski, J. (1995). "Subiektywne Znaczenie Pojecia Demokracja a Ujmowanie Rzeczywistosci Spoleczno-Politycznej." In J. Reykowski (ed.). *Potoczne Wyobrazenia o Demokracji* (pp. 19–66). Warszawa: IP PAN.

Roguska, B. (1999). "Ocena Perspektywy Polskiej Gospodarki." [Opinions on Prospects for the Polish Economy]. *CBOS,* 4, 15–32

Roguska, B. (2000b). "Obowiazki Panstwa Wobec Obywateli i Obywatela Wobec Pa?stwa." [Duties of the State Towards Citizens and Citizens Toward the State]. *CBOS,* 5: 57–74.

Roguska, B. (2000c). "Polacy, Wegrzy, Czesi, Litwini i Ukraincy o Integracji z Uni? Europejską." [Poles, Hungarians, Chechs, Lithuanians and Ukrainians on Integration With the European Union]. *CBOS* 6: 67–82.

Rose, R. (1996). "Investing in Central and Eastern Europe: Former Soviet Empire Rules out Old Regime." *Financial Times* (London), p. 5.

Salabaj, N. and Yaremenko, A. (1996). "The Social-Political Attitudes of the Ukraine Population: February 1996." National Institute of Strategic Studies in Kiev. Manuscript published at: *http://www.umich.edu/~iinet/crees/fsugrant/nat.html*)

Schuman H., Rieger Ch., and Gaidys V. (1994). "Collective Memories in the United States and Lithuania." In N. Schwarz and S. Sudman (eds.). Autobiographical Memory and the Validity of Retrospective Reports. New York: Springer-Verlag.

Sedlak, L. (1994) "Fears Over Privatization." *The Prague Post.* 29 June.

Segodnya (1997). Poll: 33 Percent of Russian Citizens Oppose the Practice of Inviting Guest Workers." 2 June, p. 2

Shavel, S. (1998). "Sotcialnaya Politika v Otnoshenii Postradavshih ot Avarii na CHAES." [Social Policy toward Victims of the Chernobyl Accident]. *Sotsic,* 8: 26–27.

Sherwell, P. (1998). "Secretive Tycoon's Poll Victory Raises Nazi Fears A Far-Right Extremist Has Found Favor with Germany's Young Jobless." *Sunday Telegraph,* 3 May, p. 29.

Shiraev, E. and Zubok, V. (2001). *Anti-Americanism in Russia: From Stalin to Putin.* N.Y.: Palgrave.

Shiraev, E. and Levy, D. (2001). *Introduction to Cross-cultural Psychology.* Needham Heights, MA: Allyn and Bacon.

Shlapentokh, V. and Matveeva, S. (1999). "Catastrofism, ili Strah pered Budushim." [Catastropism or Fear of the Future]. In V. Shlapentohk, V.Shubkin, and V.Yadov (eds.), *Katastroficheskoe Soznanie v Sovremennom Mire v Konce XX veka.* Moscow: MONF, pp. 57–77.

Shlapentokh,V. (1990). *Soviet Intellectuals and Political Power,* Princeton: Princeton University Press, 1990.

Shushkevich, S. (2000). A Presentation at the Woodrow Wilson Center, Washington DC, March 16.

Shvarov, A. (1997). "In Expectation of Mass Unrest." *Nezavisimaya Gazeta,* 26 November, p. 6.

Sidyachko, A. (1992). "Catastrophe Brings Psychosis Epidemic Survey of Psychological Effects of Chernobyl Catastrophe Produces Sensational Results." *Megapolis-Express,* April 29, p.2.

Sigel, R. (1989). "Introduction: Persistence and Change." In Sigel, R. (ed.), *Political Learning in Adulthood: A sourcebook of Theory and Research.* Chicago: The University of Chicago Press.

Smith, G. B. (1999). "The Psychological Dimension of Transition: A Stage Model" (pp. 136–154). In E. Shiraev and B. Glad (eds.), *The Russian Transformation: Political, Sociological, and Psychological Aspects.* NY: St. Martin's Press.

Snoddy, R. (2000). "Telecoms Sale in Lithuania." *The Times,* 1 May.

Sorokin, P.A. (1968). *Man and Society in Calamity: The Effects of War, Revolution, Famine, Pestilence upon Human Mind, Behavior, Social Organization, and Cultural Life.* New York: Greenwood Press.

Sotis (1999). "Integratsiya Belarusi I Rossii v Ocenkah Naseleniya." [Russian-Belarusian Integration in People's Opinion.] *Sotis,* 9: 51.

Statisticheskoie Obozrenie (1997). Data from no. 4, p. 9.

STEM (2000). "Trends 3/2000 Jak Vidíme Své Postavení Mezi Německem a Ruskem?" [How do We Perceive our Position between Germany and Russia?]. Prague: STEM.

Strzeszewski, M. (1999a). *Nadzieje i Obawy Polakow.* [Hopes and Fears of Poles]. *CBOS,* 3: 44–70.

Strzeszewski, M. (1999b). *Opinie o Sytuacji Kraju na Arenie Miedzynarodowej.* [Opinions on the International Position of Poland]. *CBOS* 6, 21–32.

Strzeszewski, M. (2000). Sytuacja Polski na Arenie Międzynarodowej w Opinii Publicznej. [Public Opinion on the International Position of Poland.] *CBOS,* 6: 46–66.

Stylinski, A. (1999). "While Most Applaud, Nationalists Warn NATO Threatens Sovereignty." *The Associated Press,* 11 March.

Szamado, E. (2001). "Anti-terror fever reaches Eastern Europe." International News. *Agence France Presse,* 3 October.

Tarm, M. (1996). "Sense of Betrayal May Topple Lithuania's Communists." *Los Angeles Times,* October 16.

The American Jewish Committee. (2000). *Russian Jewish Immigrants in New York City: Status, Identity, and Integration.* New York: AJC.

The Economist (1996). "Eastern Europe. Feeling Perkier." 2 March, p. 48.

The Guardian (1993). "Ex-Soviets Dislike Market Economy; Most Feel Respect for Rights Falling." 25 February, p. A10.

The Public Opinion Report (1999). 8 January, no. 64, p. 39–40.

The Public Opinion Foundation (1999). Survey Reports Series, March 24, no. 38, p. 19.

The World Bank (1997). *World Development Indicators.* Washington, DC: World Bank.

The World Bank (1999). *World Development Indicators.* Washington, DC: World Bank.

Titarenko, L. (1998) "SPID kak Ugroza Sotcial'noy Katastrofy" [AIDS as A Threat of Social Catastrophe]. *Sotis,* 8, 45.

Titarenko, L. Clark McPhail, and John McCarthy (1998). "Routinizing Protest Policing in the Transition from Communism: The Evolution of Social Control in Minsk, Belarus." Paper delivered at the *XIV World Congress of ISA.* Montreal, July 26–August 1.

Titarenko, L. (1999). *Public Opinion in Belarus 1999.* Washington, DC: IFES, A-1.

Toranska, T. (1989). *Oni.* Warszawa: Omnipress.

Toranska, T. (1994). *My.* Warszawa: Most.

Transparency International (1998). *Annual Report 1998. The Fight Against Corruption: Is the Tide Now Turning?*

Tretyakov, M. (1995). "Why Poles Fear Russia" *Pravda,* 10 June, p. 3.

Trickey, M. (1996). Soviet Era Returning in Belarus. *The Gazette* (Montreal) 20 November, p. F10.

Tyavlovskiy, M. (1999). "Cooperation." *Belorusskaya Delovaya Gazeta,* 17 April.

USIA (1999). "Most Belarusians See Hard Times Ahead, But Still Back Lukashenko" *Opinion Analysis,* July 22, 1999. Washington: USIA, 4 5.

USIA (1999). *The People Have Spoken: Global Views of Democracy.* A Special Report of the Office of Research and Media Reaction. Washington: USIA.

Van Der Laan, N. (1996). "Fraud Alleged as Lukashenko Claims Victory." *The Daily Telegraph,* 26 November, p. 16.

Vardomatsky A. (1999). "Nekotorie Osobennosti Post-Sovetskogo Obshestvennogo Mneniya." [Some Trends on Post-Soviet Public Opinion]. *Sotis,* no. 9, 62.

Vilmorus, R. (1997). "Baltic Data House, Saar Poll. New Baltic Barometer III: A Survey Study." *Studies in Public Policy,* vol. 284, Glasgow: Centre for the Study of Public Policy, University of Strathclyde, pp. 28- 36.

VTsIOM (1999). A poll quoted by *PolitRu,* 21 October.

Wciorka, B. (1999a). "Kto Zyskał, a Kto Stracil na Przemianach w Polsce? Jak Zyjemy Dzisiaj? [Who Profited and Who Lost out in the Transformation in Poland? How do we Live Today?]." *CBOS* 12, 77–102.

Wciorka, B. (1999b). "Jakie Sa Nasze Zarobki, a Jakie Powinny Byc?" [How Much We Earn and How Much we Should Earn?]. *CBOS* 3, 98–114.

Wciorka, B. (2000). "Nadzieje i Obawy Polakow w Roku 2000." [Hopes and Fears of Poles in 2000]. *CBOS,* 2, pp. 96–117.

Weber, B. (1992). "Many in Former Soviet Lands Say that Now, They Feel Even More Insecure." *The New York Times,* 23 April, A3.

Weber, M. (1976). *The Protestant Ethic and Spirit of Capitalism.* London: Allen and Urwin.

Wyman, M. 1997. *Public Opinion in Post-Communist Russia.* London: Macmillan Press.

Zinoskiy, V. (1999) Chislennost i Osnovnie Social'no Demograficheskie Characteristiki Naselenija Respubliki Belarus po Dannim Perepisi Naselenija 1999 Goda, Zhurnal Sociologija, no. 1, p. 11.

Index